for the Christian family

LEARNING ABOUT SEX

Love, Sex & God

For **young women**
ages **15 and up**

CONCORDIA PUBLISHING HOUSE · SAINT LOUIS

Acknowledgments

We wish to thank all medical, child development, and family life consultants who have assisted in the development, updating, and revising of the Learning About Sex series.

Copyright © 1982, 1988, 1995, 1998, 2008 Concordia Publishing House

3558 S. Jefferson Ave., St. Louis, MO 63118-3968

1-800-325-3040 · www.cph.org

From text orginally written by Bill Ameiss and Jane Graver.

Scripture quotations, unless otherwise indicated, are taken from the Holy Bible, New International Version®. NIV®. Copyright © 1973, 1978, 1984 by International Bible Society. Used by permission of Zondervan Publishing House. All rights reserved.

Scripture quotations marked ESV are from The Holy Bible, English Standard Version®. Copyright © 2001 by Crossway Bibles, a publishing ministry of Good News Publishers, Wheaton, Illinois. Used by permission. All rights reserved.

The Bible text in this publication marked TEV is from the Good News Bible, the Bible in Today's English Version. Copyright © American Bible Society 1966, 1976. Used by permission.

This publication may be available in braille, in large print, or on cassette tape for the visually impaired. Please allow 8 to 12 weeks for delivery. Write to Lutheran Blind Mission, 7550 Watson Rd., St. Louis, MO 63119-4409; call toll-free 1-888-215-2455; or visit the Web site: www.blindmission.org.

Manufactured in the United States of America

2   3   4   5   6   7   8   9   10   11   22   21   20   19   18   17   16   15   14   13

Book 5 of the
Learning About Sex series for girls,
ages 15 and older

Contents

Editors' Foreword

This book is one of a series of six designed to help parents communicate Christian values to their children in the area of sexuality. *Love, Sex, and God* is the fifth book in the series. It is written especially for young women ages 15 and older—and, of course, for the parents, teachers, and other significant grown-ups who may want to discuss the book with them.

Like its predecessor, the new Learning about Sex series provides information about the social-psychological and physiological aspects of human sexuality. Moreover, it does so from a distinctively Christian point of view, in the context of our relationship to the God who created us and redeemed us in Jesus Christ. The series presents sex as another good gift from God that is to be used responsibly.

Each book in the series is graded—in vocabulary and in the amount of information it provides. It answers the questions that persons at each age level typically ask.

Because children vary widely in their growth rates and interest levels, parents and other concerned adults will want to preview each book in the series, directing the child to the next graded book when she is ready for it.

Ideally, this book is part of a much more broadly focused yet more personal training of young people for biblical adulthood. For young women, this training can flow from a mentoring relationship similar to that of Naomi and Ruth. A young person can learn much from a mother, grandmother, or other adult who trusts in Jesus for her salvation. See the example of Eunice and Lois in 2 Timothy 1:5. In the context of such a relationship, questions of a personal nature can be asked and answered, insightful discussions held, and godly behaviors modeled.

Use this and the other books in the series to facilitate your conversations about sex and sexual issues and when answering other questions a child might have. The books in this series also can be used as mini units or as part of another course of study in a Christian school setting. Whenever the books are used in a class setting, it is important to let the parents know beforehand, since they have the prime responsibility for the sex education of their children.

While parents will appreciate the help of the school, they will want to know what is being taught. As the Christian home and the Christian school work together, Christian values in sex education can be more effectively strengthened.

The Editors

Introduction

What does it mean to be made in the image and likeness of God?

What does it take to be a young woman in today's culture?

What do I do with sexual temptation?

Is it even possible to live according to God's standard for sexual purity?

What is God's design for sexuality anyway?

These are some pretty deep questions. Most people never pause to consider these matters. Even if you have, you probably still have some confusion. Sometimes the Bible seems so clear in its guidance for our lives, and other times it is pretty hard to understand. Making matters worse, the culture offers some pretty attractive and enticing lies about what sex is all about and what it means to be a young woman in the world today.

As a young Christian woman, you are in the midst of a great deal of change. Not only is your body continuing to mature, but your mental, emotional, and spiritual capacities are growing as well. You are growing more confident, strong, and wise, but you also may struggle with self-doubt, confusion about the world, and a growing sense that there must be more to faith in Jesus Christ than what you learned in Sunday School. Complicating everything is a growing sexual desire that is both exciting and confusing. Just how are you supposed to put it all together?

The purpose of this book is to explore these and a whole range of related questions and subjects. We'll draw on the questions, struggles, and experiences of many young women as they, too, have faced the responsibilities of becoming adults. We'll try to help you use their questions and experiences together with reliable physiological information as you work through what it means to be a Christian woman, concerned about honoring God with your sexuality.

The Bible gives us the basis and the standards for our life with God, our relationships with others, and our attitudes about sex. And contrary to a common misperception, God's Word is not just a list of prohibitions designed to cramp our fun. God's plan for our lives is a glorious and exciting path that leads us to abiding joy throughout our lives and into eternity. We also are reminded that throughout all of the twists and turns life brings our way, our Savior forgives and strengthens, encourages and directs us in the new life He calls us to live for Him.

Chapter 1

Sex and Sexuality

God's Plan for Sexuality

So, what does the Bible really say about sex? Chances are, you are familiar with the commandment against committing **adultery**. You also may remember many verses expressing God's prohibition on **fornication**. You may even be familiar with St. Paul's explanation that your body is a temple of the Holy Spirit and that sexual sin is an offense not just against God but against your own body.

Okay, you say, but I have also read throughout the Bible about people committing all kinds of sexual sin, even King David, whom many have called "a man after God's own heart." There is even a prostitute among Jesus' human ancestors. So, which is it: Does God really care if I follow His standards for sexuality, or can I ignore them like so many people in the Bible did?

Jesus Himself sheds some light on this seeming disparity in Matthew 19. Some Pharisees tested Jesus by asking Him a hard question about divorce. Jesus responded by reminding them that God created humans as male and female and designed them for sexual and spiritual oneness in marriage. The Pharisees persisted and asked why Moses allowed them to divorce. Jesus replied, "Moses permitted you to divorce your wives because your hearts were hard. But it was not this way from the beginning" (Matthew 19:8).

Isn't it interesting how the Pharisees confused what was common in the sinful world with the way God designed things to be? Jesus quickly pointed out this foolishness. Twice in that conversation, He pointed His questioners back to God's design in the beginning. The truth is that God does have a standard for sexual purity, which He proclaims throughout the Bible. But because of sin, people have corrupted God's design and tried to take matters into their own hands. Have you noticed that sexual sin in the Bible is never excused? There are always serious consequences.

In order to grasp what God's plan for our sexuality is, let's take Jesus' suggestion and go back to the beginning before sin twisted and distorted what God made to be good.

Sin Enters the Picture

Sexuality was part of God's plan from the very beginning. In Genesis 1–2, the Bible tells us that God made the man, Adam, first. Then recognizing that Adam was lonely, God caused a deep sleep to fall upon Adam. Taking one of Adam's ribs, God fashioned Eve, the first woman. He made the first man and the first woman to complete and complement each other. They lived in harmony, unity, and in close and perfect communication with each other and with God. Together they enjoyed an ideal existence in the Garden of Eden.

But the complete happiness of our first parents was not long to last. Satan tempted them and, rather than resisting, they sinned, placing themselves and all of creation into the devil's firm grasp. Still, God did not abandon those He had created in His image. He called out to Adam and then to Eve, asking them what they had done. Pronouncing punishment, God also included the promise of the Savior. God identified the pain of childbirth as a consequence of the woman's sin and placed Eve under the authority of her husband. He directed Adam to the pain and frustration of both work and responsibility that would result from the fall. Adam and Eve and all the men and women who would follow after them would know disappointment, hardship, and heartache as results of the fall into sin. Sin would contaminate every aspect of their lives, including self-image, personal fulfillment and satisfaction, and relationships with both God and others.

God's people do not always follow His plan for their lives perfectly, but isn't it amazing that God receives us into His family in spite of our sin? He does this for Christ's sake, who died on the cross for our forgiveness. God desires that we obey Him—this is how we are to show our love for Him—but He is quick to forgive and restore us when we fall.

The other side of sin involves our redemption in and through Christ.

The Bible calls us to be transformed into the likeness of Christ. (See 2 Corinthians 3:18.) This is only possible when the Holy Spirit lives within us and daily works in us the process of sanctification. When Paul writes about living holy lives, including sexual purity, he is not taunting us with some impossible task or trying to lay new burdens on us. He is actually describing the newness of life in Christ, where we have been freed to love Him and others as God designed.

This isn't to say it's easy, but all of life requires discipleship, including living out our sexuality. The first step in that discipleship is learning to live as a Christian woman—a fallen but redeemed woman in Christ.

Is Being Male or Female Really That Important?

This may seem like a strange question, but some people really wonder if there is such a big difference. Our culture has been pushing the idea that masculinity and femininity are just a social construct—or, to put it another way, that our gender is created by society's attitudes and has no deeper meaning.

The Bible affirms that men and women have equal worth in God's eyes, but it is also clear that we are very different by design. It's not just that males and females have different sexual organs—this much is obvious—it's that our entire makeup is different. Research shows that men and women process information differently, have different physical strengths and weaknesses, and approach relationships differently.

Contrary to some fashionable but very incorrect philosophies being floated today, you began to be a female at the instant of conception. After a significant sonogram or at your birth, your parents joyfully said, "It's a girl!" From that moment on, everyone treated you as a girl. By the age of two, you were watching other females very carefully so you could imitate their femininity in walk, mannerisms, and speech. For as long as you live, you will experience life as a female. Your gender is central to who you are. It isn't just a trendy social idea past its prime. The gender blurring we see in culture today is yet again a human twisting of God's good design.

Unfortunately, the way we understand ourselves as females and the way we relate to ourselves, to God, to males, and to other females has been negatively affected by sin. We often act harshly toward others, even talking and acting disrespectfully to the men and women around us. We shake our fist at God when He won't condone our doing whatever feels good. And we have wounds deep inside of us—loneliness, anger, lust, sorrow—because we choose not to follow God's Word.

A way to describe this situation we all face is "disintegration." We are disintegrated beings, disconnected from God, from others, and even from ourselves. Did you ever wonder why even a Christian as great as St. Paul struggled to do what he didn't want to do and didn't do what he wanted to do? (See Romans 7:14–25.) Sin has fractured the harmony among our bodies, minds, and spirits.

But Jesus came to live, die, and rise again for all human sin. He came to break down the walls of hostility that separate us from God and from one another. He came to restore in each of us—either male or female— the "new self, which is being renewed in knowledge in the image of its Creator" (Colossians 3:10).

In a very real sense, Jesus came to "reintegrate" us. He restores us to a loving relationship with God our Father. He heals the age-old strife between men and women. He brings forgiveness and grace to marriages and relationships between parents and children. He even helps us align our desires with His, bringing back the harmony among our bodies, minds, and spirits, including our sexual desires.

The Deeper Meaning of Sex and Marriage

The big question for many Christians is not, Should I follow God's plan for sexual purity? but, What does such a plan look like? Another common question, especially for Christian young people, is, How far can I go without sinning? Does this describe your attitude concerning sex?

Have you ever read through the entire Bible? It's a challenge to be sure, but so rewarding. For instance, if you haven't read the entire Bible, you probably didn't notice that the story of God's people begins in Genesis with the marriage of a man and a woman and ends in Revelation with the marriage of the Lamb and the Bride, also known as the marriage between Christ and all His believers, the Church.

What's even more interesting is that throughout the Old Testament, one of the ways God describes the relationship He has with His people is in terms of a marriage. He calls Himself the Bridegroom, and Israel is His Bride. He also laments when Israel strays, just as a husband would weep over an unfaithful wife.

It gets even clearer in the New Testament. Not only did Jesus teach on marriage, He also used the same marital imagery when speaking to His followers. Do you recall when He said His disciples did not fast because they were with the Bridegroom? (See Matthew 9:14–16.) Later, St. Paul wrote about Jesus' work of giving Himself up for the Church in order to make her holy as a Bride for Himself.

If you've ever attended a wedding, chances are you heard Ephesians 5 being read. In this chapter, Paul compares earthly marriages and the love between a man and a woman with the love Christ has for His Church. And there are many more examples.

Is it possible that all this marital imagery scattered throughout the Bible is God's way of telling us something important about Himself and our relationship to Him?

In Genesis 1, we read, "Then God said, 'Let us make man in our image, in our likeness . . . .' So God created man in His own image, in the image of God He created him; male and female He created them. God blessed them and said to them, 'Be fruitful and increase in number; fill the earth and subdue it'" (Genesis 1:26–28).

When Adam awoke from the sleep God caused and saw Eve for the first time, he said, "This is now bone of my bones and flesh of my flesh" (Genesis 2:23). Adam recognized that the woman was like him but also very different—one to complement and complete him.

Being made in God's image and likeness involved being created male and female—distinct persons, but called into oneness in marriage. From this oneness, God planned for new life to emerge as Adam and Eve were to join together in love and bring forth children. God's love also leads to new life. He created us and gives us new life in Christ out of His great love for us.

Why would God create us this way? It's dangerous to speculate on God's reasons for doing anything, but when we look at the entirety of the Bible and its consistent theme of marriage—that most intimate of human relationships—it almost appears that He was trying to give us a glimpse of our eternal destiny with Him in heaven. Put simply, God loves us all and desires that we share eternal life with Him in heaven. He is using an earthly physical relationship to help us understand the depth of His spiritual love for us.

How Does That Affect My Sexual Desires Now?

This heavenly picture has everything to do with love, sex, and marriage for you as a young Christian woman. We are made in God's image, not the other way around—His love for us can provide daily guidance as we navigate our own sexual desires in a sinful world.

In the coming chapters, you will learn more about God's wonderful design for sex, relationships, and marriage, guided by this positive vision of being made to share in and give God's love to others.

If living this out seems difficult or even impossible at this point, remember that it is not our efforts that save us; it is Christ alone living in us and working through us that allows us to conform our desires to His will. This process will require understanding and embracing what it means to be a young Christian woman in a world often incompatible—even hostile—to such a calling.

Chapter 2

The Female and the Male Sexual Systems

One of the most remarkable examples of how wonderfully and intricately we were made occurs right in our own bodies. Have you ever paused to wonder at your own body? Maybe you have felt uncomfortable with yourself, especially during puberty and adolescence. This is natural but also unfortunate. As a teenager, you may have been very self-conscious about starting your period, changes in your breasts, or having these changes occur earlier or later than your friends. The truth is that almost every young person feels uncomfortable with herself or himself at some point.

However, there is a danger if you allow your discomfort to become a kind of hatred or even a disappointment with your body. We know our bodies aren't perfect because of the effects of sin, but we also know that God was directly involved in our creation. He made us who we are!

Do you blame God for what you look like—the color of your hair or eyes, whether you are tall or short, thick or thin? Did God make a mistake with you? It might be tempting to think so, but God knew what He was doing, and He loves you as you are.

It is tempting to just look at the outside of a person and think he is really strong, or she is really cute, but beneath the surface, we are all "fearfully and wonderfully made" (Psalm 139:14). Don't think so? Consider your eyes that allow you to read this book or your brain that helps you translate the words on this page into meaning. What about the breath you just took? You didn't even have to think about it, yet it happened. When you take time to look at all the amazing systems in your body, you can see that it is truly awesome.

This is no less true for your reproductive system and sexual organs. You may not even think much about this part of your body, but it is just as amazingly designed as the rest of you.

The Female Sexual System

For from Him and through Him and to Him are all things.
Romans 11:36

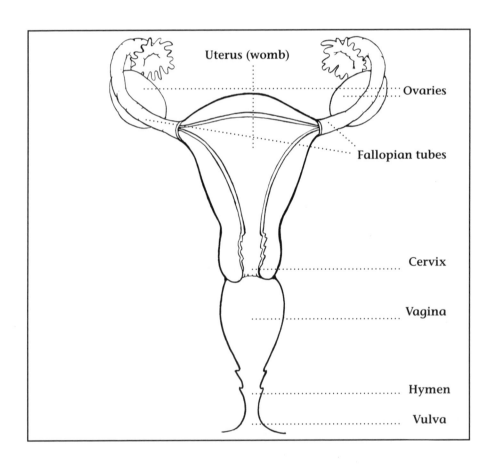

The Internal Sexual Organs

A sign of God's wonderful design is the difference between male and female sexual organs. Whereas most of the male reproductive system is outside the body, most of the female reproductive system is inside the body.

Deep inside the female body is a pair of **ovaries**. They contain thousands of undeveloped egg cells. When a girl is somewhere between the ages of 9 and 16, her ovaries begin to produce **estrogen**, the female **hormone** that controls many changes in her body.

During the next few years, her breasts develop and her hips broaden. Her height and weight increase rapidly. And her **sex organs** grow. Hair appears under her arms and in her pubic area. As **menstruation** begins, she may also notice a clear whitish discharge from her **vagina**.

At **puberty,** the egg cells in the ovaries begin to ripen. About once every 28 days, a ripe egg cell bursts out of the **follicle** that has nourished it and leaves the ovary. The ripe egg is swept into the nearby **fallopian tube** by fluids and tiny hairlike **cilia** on the inside of the tube. **Fertilization**, the uniting of a mature egg cell with a sperm cell, when it happens, almost always happens in the fallopian tube. Immediately the covering of the egg cell changes to block the entry of other sperm. The new cell that has been created moves slowly into the **uterus**.

In a mature woman, the uterus is about the size and shape of a large pear. The walls of the uterus are made of extremely elastic muscles, able to stretch to an enormous size during **pregnancy**. These same powerful muscles contract downwards to make childbirth possible. They also contract during menstruation, sometimes causing cramps in some women.

The vagina, or birth passageway, is a tube also made of elastic muscle. The walls of the vagina touch each other most of the time, much like a collapsed balloon. During sexual excitement, the vagina expands and produces a lubricating fluid that makes **intercourse** easier.

The **cervix**, or neck of the uterus, which opens into the vagina, is made of muscles that close tightly during pregnancy but stretch enormously during childbirth. No human engineer could design such a perfect system for beginning and supporting a new life! It's another miracle by God, the master Designer!

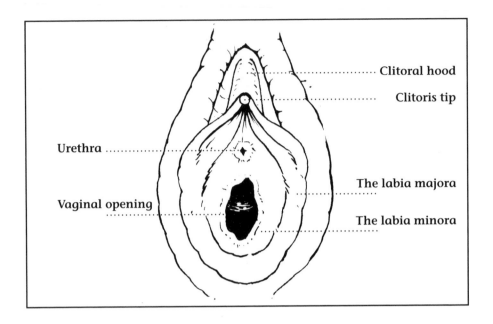

Clitoral hood

Clitoris tip

Urethra

The labia majora

Vaginal opening

The labia minora

The Vulva, or External Sexual Organs

The opening of the vagina is partly covered by the **hymen**, a membrane that is broken the first time sexual intercourse occurs. At one time, an unbroken hymen was an important proof that a girl was a **virgin**. We now know that it often is broken much earlier in life without the girl realizing it.

Surrounding the opening to the vagina are two fatty folds of skin, the labia majora (major lips). The outer sides are covered with hair. They serve as protection for the genital area.

Inside these are two more folds of skin, the labia minora (minor lips). Sometimes they are hidden by the major lips; sometimes they stick out between them. They may be pink or brown, wrinkled or smooth.

At the top of the labia minora is a small cylinder of very sensitive tissue, the **clitoris**. A woman may be able to see the pea-sized end of it with a mirror, or it may be hidden by the folds of the labia.

Between the clitoris and the vagina is the **urethra**, where urine leaves the body. It is very small and is completely separate from the vagina.

Menstruation

Which of the following common myths have you heard?

1. Menstruation is dirty because bad blood is leaving the body.

2. Menstruation is an illness. A menstruating woman should avoid exercise, especially swimming.

3. The menstrual cramps some women complain about are imaginary.

4. Women cannot handle important jobs because their menstrual cycle produces mood changes and uneven levels of energy.

The above statements are *all false.* Don't be embarrassed if you have fallen for one or more of them. They are so widely believed that nearly everyone is affected by the attitudes they represent. Because there is a kernel of truth in each of them, you need detailed, factual information to separate the truth from the myth. Here it is:

Facts about Myth 1: The menstrual flow is a mixture of blood and cell fragments. When a ripe cell leaves the ovary, the uterus prepares for the possible beginning of a new life. Hormones (**estrogen** and **progesterone**) cause a soft thick lining to form on the uterus walls. Extra blood flows to the uterus, ready to nourish a fertilized egg.

When fertilization does not happen, the egg cell, the new lining, and the extra blood are not needed. They break up and flow out through the vagina. This process happens about once a month for 25–40 years. Since God makes every person unique, the menstrual cycle is a little different for each woman.

Although menstruation is a normal, healthy process, some girls are embarrassed by it, especially in the early years. This feeling usually changes when they become more used to their adult bodies.

Perhaps the "dirty" label began because of the odor that forms when air and warmth interact with the menstrual flow. If a woman keeps herself clean and changes sanitary napkins or tampons frequently, odor will not be a problem.

Facts about Myth 2: Menstruation is a sign of a healthy, normal body. Although many women have times when they feel uncomfortable during their periods, they can and should carry on normal activities. Most women feel best if they exercise moderately rather than strenuously.

Following ordinary health rules is especially important at this time: get enough rest, drink plenty of fluids, and avoid salt to prevent fluid retention.

Facts about Myth 3: Menstrual pain is real but not universal. For some women, hormonal changes just before menstruation produce a variety of symptoms called premenstrual syndrome (PMS). The most common are a dull abdominal ache, a feeling of fullness, and breast tenderness. Women who notice PMS symptoms should cut down on salt, sugar, and caffeine during the week before menstruation.

Studies show that daily exercise will give definite relief to about two-thirds of the women who suffer from menstrual pain. The removal of tension also helps.

Facts about Myth 4: Other symptoms of PMS may include tension, depression, or fatigue. Many women feel extra energy or exceptionally happy midway between two menstrual periods, when a mature egg leaves the ovary. The extra hormones produced at that time can boost her energy level and make her feel good all over. Two weeks later her hormone level drops—just before she begins to menstruate. She may feel tired and somewhat depressed. However, there are other body cycles that have a similar effect—and these apply to men as well as women. We all need to learn about ourselves and to adjust to these changes and make the most of every day.

The Male Sexual System

For from Him and through Him and to Him are all things.
Romans 11:36

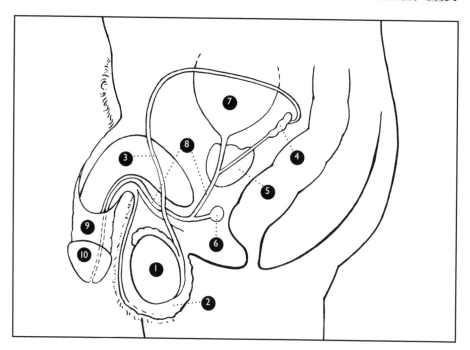

The Male Reproductive Organs:

1. Testicles

2. Scrotum

3. Vas Deferens

4. Seminal Vesicles

5. Prostate Gland

6. Cowper's Glands

7. Bladder

8. Urethra

9. Penis

10. Glans

The Testicles

The **testicles** are roundish glands that hang just behind the penis in a pouch called the **scrotum**. Why is the left testicle lower (and sometimes larger) than the right one? Is this a mistake in God's creation? No—it's really a miracle of design, for it keeps the testicles from getting hurt as the legs come together.

Consider, too, God's wisdom in putting the testicles in the scrotum—*outside* the rest of the body. In this way the testicles are able to maintain the temperature they need—about 4 degrees lower than the rest of the body. In cold weather, the muscles of the scrotum contract to bring the testicles close to the body. In warm weather, the muscles relax to lower the testicles away from the body. In this way the testicles are always kept near the proper temperature.

A boy's testicles are inside his body until a few weeks before he is born. Then the testicles descend into the scrotum. In about 3 percent of baby boy births, one or both testicles do not come out into the scrotum. Although a doctor's help is needed to correct this condition, these boys are usually normal in every other way. Actually, only one functioning testicle is necessary for producing sperm and hormones.

The testicles produce **sperm**, tiny cells that are needed for reproduction. From puberty into old age, these amazing glands make millions of sperm a day. Sperm can be seen only through a microscope; one drop of seminal fluid can contain 120 million of them. They look like tadpoles with skinny, active tails.

Another important job of the testicles is to produce **testosterone**, a hormone or chemical that controls the development of male sex characteristics—like a beard and lower voice. During puberty, boys notice that the testicles and **penis** grow and become darker in color; hair grows in the **pubic** area and later on the body and face; the voice deepens; muscles and bones grow very rapidly. Suddenly boys are interested in girls in a new and exciting way.

The Sperm Storage and Transportation System

After sperm are produced in tiny tubes inside the testicles, they move to larger tubes, where they mature. Then they travel through another tube (the **vas deferens**) to the **seminal vesicles**, which are two pouches just behind the **bladder**. Next to the seminal vesicles is an active little gland, the **prostate**. It constantly manufactures a fluid that mixes with fluids from other glands to make **semen**. Semen is the white, sticky fluid in which sperm leave the penis. Only 1–3 teaspoons of semen leave the body at any one time.

The Penis

The penis hangs in front of the testicles. Like the testicles, the penis is very sensitive to contact. The **glans**, the end of the penis, is especially sensitive. It is covered with a loose elastic skin, the **foreskin**.

Many doctors recommend **circumcision** (removing the foreskin) to prevent dirt or urine from collecting under the foreskin and thus causing infection. Usually this simple operation is done soon after birth, but it can be done at any age. Circumcision does not affect a male's ability to give or receive sexual pleasure. Some parents choose not to have this procedure performed. With or without the foreskin, the penis functions the same way.

Erections

When a man is sexually aroused, the soft, limp tissue of his penis becomes erect and larger—hard enough to stand away from the body. Even though there is a difference in the size and shape of penises, there is little difference in the sexual satisfaction for either man or woman.

The inside of a penis is a lot like a sponge. During an erection extra blood rushes into the penis. Valves close to hold this blood under pressure.

Erections can happen at any age, but they seem to happen more often during **adolescence**. They can be caused by sexual feelings and daydreams, but they also occur because of tight clothing, pressure from a full bladder—or even for no apparent reason. Although it can be very embarrassing when it happens in public, it is usually not very noticeable to other people.

Ejaculation

If the stimulation that causes an erection is continued, semen moves into the urethra tube. Strong muscles move it along until it squirts or oozes from the penis. This **ejaculation**, or squirting out of semen, goes along with intense feelings of pleasure, called an **orgasm**. Although semen and urine both leave the body through the urethra, they cannot pass through the penis at the same time. Special muscles close off the bladder when the penis is erect.

When the seminal vesicles are full, ejaculation may take place during sleep. This is called a **nocturnal emission** or **wet dream** because of the sex dream that may happen during the ejaculation.

Sometimes young men feel guilt or embarrassment about nocturnal emissions, but they are completely natural. They are part of God's design for relieving sexual tensions and releasing surplus semen.

Common Questions

What happens when a woman's vagina is too small for a man's penis? (Jenny, 16)

The walls of the vagina are elastic enough to permit the birth of a baby; an erect penis is much smaller. When a woman is sexually aroused, her vagina gets bigger and produces a fluid that lubricates the inner walls.

Why do some people masturbate? (Melissa, 16)

Masturbation is common among both males and females. Touching the penis or the clitoris or **vulva** can produce strong feelings of pleasure. When a person touches herself to produce those feelings of pleasure, it is called self-stimulation or masturbation.

Some people maintain there is nothing wrong with masturbating, and others think it is harmful or sinful. What do you think? Although in the past, stories were told to frighten youth away from this practice, most of those were not true.

So, what is true? Consider this: When a person masturbates, he or she usually also thinks sexual thoughts about another person or maybe recalls sexual images stored in the brain from pornography use. While the Bible doesn't specifically speak about masturbation, it does strongly condemn lusting after others. Jesus went so far as to say that lusting after another person is the same as committing adultery.

Some might say that they are able to masturbate without looking at pornography or lusting. Is it wrong then? Well, consider again God's good design. He made males and females to complement one another and designed their sexual organs to work together to produce new life. Nowhere in the Bible does God instruct us to live for ourselves. This seems to hold true for our sexuality as well. One concern about masturbation is that it can easily become habit-forming. If masturbation becomes a habit, then a person is actually conditioning herself or himself to receive sexual pleasure apart from another person. (Not only that, but for males, the nerve endings in the penis may become desensitized through continual masturbation so that he may have trouble enjoying intercourse with his wife later in life.)

People often masturbate as a release or a way to escape their problems. That's also why some people use drugs. They find a distraction to take them away from their feelings of worthlessness, pain, or depression. In such situations, these people would be encouraged to stop using something else to hide their problems and go to God and others who love them to help them deal with those problems.

This would be an example of the disintegration we spoke about earlier. Rather than continuing a practice that separates us from others or keeps us confused inside, we can always turn to Jesus to help reintegrate our lives.

We can be assured that He desires to help us control our sexual desires but also that His forgiveness is quick when we fail.

Will masturbation cause problems later in intercourse? (Sharika, 17)

There's more to intercourse than bringing body parts together. In the sexual fantasies that usually go with masturbation, someone of the other sex is used as a toy for your sexual pleasure. That's not much help in learning to see that someone as a valuable person who can give and receive love. Another problem: When people learn to reach orgasm very quickly through masturbation, they may have difficulty with premature orgasm in normal sexual intercourse.

You might ask yourself a question here: "Do I want to masturbate after I am married?" If you don't, consider what you are doing now to prepare for that. If you are regularly masturbating now, how will things be different once you are married? You may think that once you have a husband, all your sexual desires will be only for him. The reality is that if your sexual desires as a single person are focused on giving yourself pleasure, they will stay that way once you are married. What you do now has great impact on what you do later in life.

Learning to control your sexual desires is not easy, but a good word to help you understand what this entails is also an old word that has fallen out of favor in modern society: **chastity**. This word means to keep oneself pure. Unlike **abstinence**, chastity doesn't end once you get married. Just because you have a husband doesn't mean you can then become sexually impure. You will still need to approach your husband with pure motives and work for his good, rather than using him merely for your own needs.

One of the greatest and deepest joys you may have will be the pure, intense, and self-giving love you can share with your spouse. This may not occur if you practice self-serving love as a young woman.

I'm flat-chested, but my friend, Rosa, has large breasts. Is there something wrong with me? (Elaina, 14)

Sexual changes are triggered by each person's individual time clock. Because of this, some 14-year-olds look like adults while others, equally normal, look like children.

Even after she has finished growing, Elaina may have smaller breasts than some of her other female friends. All of us are different. Many of us are dissatisfied, too, with some of our physical characteristics until we realize that we are lovable and loving people just as we are. God has made us different physically just as He has given us different abilities.

Why do so many people think the sexual parts of our bodies are dirty? (Kimi, 15)

Ignorance, mostly. Or maybe they haven't stopped to think about how precisely, how wonderfully, each of us is made. No wonder God thought our bodies good enough to be temples of His Spirit! He made them that way. Adam and Eve were able to be completely naked and unashamed before the fall into sin. Since the fall, we have felt differently about our bodies and have had more difficulty seeing them as the gifts of God they really are.

Our culture really impacts our perceptions of our own bodies and sexuality. Even though the culture seems to worship sex, it really debases it. Women are often portrayed as sexually permissive and as objects for men's sexual desires. This degrades everyone's views of women, even for women themselves. Men often believe the culture's lies that masculinity requires bedding many women and being able to have sex for hours at a time.

Even some Christians are confused about sex. Earlier we talked about what God's Word says about sex, that it isn't just a list of rules to kill our fun. Sadly, sometimes well-meaning Christians give the impression that sex is dirty by refusing to talk about it, even with their children in appropriate ways. The parents likely mean well and are just uncomfortable, but children can inadvertently get the impression that sex is something taboo and view it in the same way as other taboo subjects.

Chapter 4 will discuss some of the ways the culture lies about sex, and it will encourage you to reclaim a godly understanding.

Chapter 3

Sex and Your Health

Despite God's glorious design for sex and relationships, many people think they can sidestep this plan and suffer no consequences. Why wouldn't they? Nearly everything in pop culture encourages people to do what feels good, to serve themselves, and to have fun no matter what. But this is not what God created us for.

Confusion about God's plan for our lives trickles down into confusion about our sexuality. Have you ever heard anyone say (or thought yourself) any of the following statements?

I need to have intercourse soon to get experience. What if I get married and can't do it right?

I'm too fat to be lovable.

A few beers make me an irresistible lover. I hear that marijuana is better yet.

It doesn't hurt to experiment a little with sniffing, smoking, popping pills, and drinking.

It's no one else's business if I choose to smoke; after all, it's MY body.

Nice people don't get STDs.

You probably don't believe any of these myths. But they are so common—and so dangerous—that we all need up-to-date information about each of them.

Inexperience

Myth 1: *I need to have intercourse soon to get experience. What if I get married and can't do it right?*

Some young people may worry unnecessarily about not being able to "do it right" when the time comes. But most of the time that is an excuse.

People do learn how to have intercourse through practice—but two inexperienced married people can learn together. They do improve with practice—considerate, mutually satisfying practice, which is difficult to have outside the security of marriage, and which God forbids outside of marriage.

Deeply satisfying sexual relationships are far more than just physical couplings. They involve rich emotional, mental, and spiritual bonds between two people who have pledged to give themselves in love to each other. Such bonds cannot truly form outside of marriage. To try to replicate this outside of marriage is to say to another person, "I kind of like you and would like to use you for a while." If a young man were that honest with a young woman, what do you think she'd do? Most of us would never be that crass, but if we try to experience sexual activity outside of marriage, that's precisely what we are saying.

Overweight

Myth 2: *I'm too fat for anyone to love me.*

To be lovable, a person really needs to be loving. God daily gives you the power to be a loving person when He pours out His limitless, unconditional love for you. In Jesus, His Son, He forgives you and calls you His own child.

However, people who are heavier than average often feel so self-conscious that it is very hard for them to take the risk of reaching out to other people.

Eating disorders are a common problem among young people today; they starve themselves or overeat compulsively or both. The current fad for skinny models sends the message that a sexy and desirable body must be slim. Not true! Good-looking people come in many shapes and sizes. Good health is attractive; dull eyes and hollow cheeks are not.

One thing that happens as people mature is that they learn to put less emphasis on physical appearance in rating themselves and others. Think about the happy, well-loved adults whom you know. How many of them look like magazine models?

The basic problem is not whether someone is of a large, medium, or small build, but how she feels about herself. She needs to remember that since God truly loves her, she has good reason to love herself. In the power of God's love for her, she can take responsibility for her own happiness. She can decide to think and do whatever lifts her up, instead of constantly putting herself down.

Overweight people may think they are alone in feeling self-conscious, but even the cheerleaders, the jocks, and those in the so-called "cool" crowd often feel as self-conscious about themselves as anyone else. We all need to realize that "before the world was made, God had already chosen us to be his through our union with Christ" (Ephesians 1:4 TEV). When we believe and accept God's love for us, we can begin to accept and love ourselves no matter how we look on the outside.

Reaching out to others who share your problem is often a big help if you are trying to turn your life around. Not all people with weight problems have an eating disorder. Many folks are influenced by genetic factors. However if you do struggle with this, ask your doctor to recommend an eating disorder clinic. Look up Overeaters Anonymous or Weight Watchers in the phone book; ask whether a teen would feel comfortable in the group nearest you. Ask about cost too. The clinic may be covered by insurance; Overeaters Anonymous is free.

Another point to remember is that eating is not the problem. The person struggling with food or other addictive behavior, including those involving pornography or drugs, has a deeper wound. Possibly just beginning healthier habits and surrounding yourself with people who love you can go a long way to helping you change, but sometimes the problem runs so deep that only a trained counselor can help you get to it. Just as you go to your parents or pastor for spiritual guidance, a Christian counselor can help you with compulsive behaviors.

One more point. If you ask God to help you change your eating habits, you may feel even more guilty if you fall off your diet. You might say to yourself: My faith isn't strong enough. God knows how hard it is for you; He forgives all kinds of failures in our lives. He will give you the power to forgive yourself and like yourself no matter what size you are. His love for you has nothing to do with how much you weigh. If you decide that dieting is not for you, that decision has no effect on your relationship with Him. Fat or thin, you will always be a valuable person in His sight.

Alcohol and Drugs

Myth 3: *A few beers make me an irresistible lover. I hear that marijuana is better yet.*

Alcohol

Establishing a happy physical and emotional relationship with another person is not easy. It's not surprising that people are anxious to believe that alcohol or drugs will help make it easier. But medical evidence shows that alcohol is not a stimulant; it is a depressant. Why does a drinker imagine she is being pepped up when she is really being slowed down?

Alcohol works first on the brain area that controls judgment and thought. The drinker is more relaxed, thinks fuzzily, and has difficulty making decisions.

If a person wants to trap someone—or be trapped—into making a choice she would not make while thinking clearly, he may encourage that person to consume alcohol. However, most of us would rather not begin a new relationship of any kind under those circumstances.

God's Word reminds Christians that we don't need to get drunk. We have a better alternative: "Do not get drunk with wine, which will only ruin you; instead, be filled with the Spirit" (Ephesians 5:18 TEV).

Marijuana

Many people incorrectly believe that marijuana is a sexual stimulant. What it really does is distort a person's picture of reality. Anything that a user believes is true becomes temporarily real for him or her.

Ephesians 5:18 is also a good text to remember when you're faced with the temptation to use marijuana or any other harmful drug.

If you are tempted to try drugs or alcohol, carefully consider the following question: is your life devoted to God or to yourself? Using marijuana only serves self, often at the expense of others. Alcohol use is often the same. Engaging in activities that may tempt us to sin takes us farther away from God. The mark of a true Christian woman is her mature faith demonstrated by service to God and to others. This kind of strong faith takes training and time. Are you working toward such a life of faith or away from it?

Addiction

Myth 4: *It doesn't hurt to experiment a little with sniffing, smoking, popping pills, and drinking.*

Nobody ever intends to become addicted to a drug. People plan to experiment a little and then walk away. It works for some. We all know someone who decided one day to quit smoking and has never looked back. Unfortunately, we also know people who have tried many times to escape from an addiction; they succeed for a while and then slip back into the old habit.

Genetic research shows that some of us are more likely to become alcoholics than others. There has been much less study of the links between genetic factors and addiction to tobacco and other drugs. However, the available evidence suggests that the same **genes** might also make a person more vulnerable to other addictions. At this time there is no way to find out whether you are a person who is extra vulnerable to alcohol or other drugs.

Roughly 50 percent of the forces that say yes or no to addiction are provided by environment and by one's own decisions. The people who are most likely to have an alcohol or drug problem are those who feel they need to drink or use another drug to help them through difficult situations. You may have heard people say:

• I feel so self-conscious at parties. When I'm drinking, I can talk to anybody.

• I smoke pot to escape the pressures of my life, the problems I have at home and at school.

• When I drink, I don't care about my worries.

We all have pain in our lives. We all have times when we feel lonely or stupid or afraid. Learning to cope with those painful feelings takes time and effort and a continual turning to Jesus. Chemical crutches do not help in the long run.

Again, when there is pain or sorrow or embarrassment in your life, remember the idea of being disintegrated. Examine your thoughts, emotions, and behaviors to find out what is driving you to seek out unhealthy activities. Once you identify what the problem is, you can focus your prayers by asking Jesus to reintegrate you again. He will help you find the guidance and support you need.

And remember that you are not alone. Others are struggling with the same feelings, even though they wear carefree masks. Jesus was an adolescent once. He had temptations, fears, and growing pains too. He understands how you feel. You can talk to Him about it and ask Him to help you. You can depend on His help as you strive to face your problems.

Drugs and Unborn Children

Myth 5: *It's no one else's business if I choose to smoke; after all, it's MY body.*

Your body is a gift from God. If you choose to, you can shut Him out of your life.

But the secret of enjoying your body is to give it back! St. Paul urges us to "offer your bodies as living sacrifices, holy and pleasing to God—this is your spiritual act of worship. Do not conform any longer to the pattern of this world, but be transformed" (Romans 12:1–2).

If you are taking anything away from this book so far, hopefully it is this: We were not made for isolation but for community. Sex is not done in isolation, nor are drugs. Everything we do has an impact on others. You may not want to be saddled with this responsibility, but God truly made us to be relational people and desires that we form healthy bonds with others. The choices you make today greatly impact your future life. It's not just that you could get very sick or die from drug or alcohol use, it's also that it trains you to approach life by ignoring the consequences of your actions. As has been said earlier, you are either in training to serve yourself or to serve God and others. If you want a happy life, consider which path is more likely to bring you lasting joy.

Also, consider the example you are making for others. You need to know what effects drugs and alcohol can have specifically on a woman's body.

A **fetus** gets the food and oxygen it needs from its mother's body. If harmful chemicals are present in her body, the fetus receives them too. If the mother is addicted to a drug, such as cocaine or crack, the newborn baby also will be addicted.

Babies of mothers who drink heavily often are born with fetal alcohol syndrome, a condition that limits both mental and emotional development. Doctors advise mothers not to drink at all during pregnancy.

In the past, sole emphasis was placed on the pregnant woman with regard to the harmful consequences of the use of alcohol, tobacco, and other drugs for the child she was carrying. Recent studies suggest, however, that fathers exposed to alcohol, tobacco, and other drugs prior to conceiving a child can produce sperm affected in such a way as to hamper or jeopardize the health of the child resulting from the union of that sperm and the egg of the mother. Therefore, chemicals consumed by either parent can have a harmful effect on the child they conceive.

Sexually Transmitted Diseases

Myth 6: *Nice people don't get STDs.*

What are STDs?

Sexually transmitted diseases, or **STDs**, are diseases that are usually passed from one person to another by close sexual contact.

The most serious STDs are **AIDS, gonorrhea, syphilis, genital herpes, chlamydia, trichomoniasis**, and **human papilloma virus** (HPV). Although a yeast infection can be passed on by sexual contact, it is not considered an STD because it has many other possible causes.

Why are STDs dangerous?

- People may have an STD without realizing it.

- Infected people are misled when symptoms disappear temporarily. However, the symptoms usually come back worse than before.

- Some consequences of untreated STDs are blindness, arthritis, mental illness, sterility, cancer, or death.

- Babies born from an infected mother may have major birth defects.

How does a person get an STD?

The bacteria, viruses, or parasites that cause STDs live on the warm, damp surfaces of the body. The diseases are most often spread by intercourse or intimate sexual activity in which these surfaces touch each other.

Because the **HIV** (AIDS) virus also lives in blood, HIV can be spread through contaminated needles used for "shooting" drugs. In the 1980s, a few people caught HIV through blood transfusions. Today's testing methods make it almost impossible to get HIV in this way. AIDS cannot be passed on by ordinary social contact such as handshakes or hugs.

Babies can be born with AIDS, syphilis, or genital herpes. Syphilis can be caught by kissing a person who has contagious mouth sores. Gonorrhea can be caught by touching infected sexual organs if one's hand has a break in the skin. Trichomoniasis can be passed on by moist towels, bathing suits, or a damp toilet seat. In all these cases, the infected person may not ever realize that he or she has an STD and can pass it on to others.

How can I tell if someone has an STD?

You can't. Only a well-informed doctor can tell. A person with a contagious case of an STD may appear perfectly healthy. On the other hand, the symptoms described in the section on STD specifics have many other possible causes. You could do someone a great injustice if you assume that his or her illness is caused by an STD.

STD Specifics

AIDS

What are the symptoms? (All people may not notice all symptoms.)

Most people have no early symptoms. The human immunodeficiency virus (HIV) that causes acquired immune deficiency syndrome (AIDS) attacks a person's immune system and damages his or her ability to fight disease. Without a functioning immune system, the person becomes vulnerable to many life-threatening illnesses, such as meningitis, pneumonia, and cancer. Symptoms of these "opportunistic" diseases include persistent cough and fever associated with shortness of breath or difficulty in breathing and multiple purplish blotches and bumps on the skin. Early symptoms may include fever, diarrhea, weight loss, tiredness, and swollen lymph glands.

How soon do the first symptoms appear?

A few weeks to 10 years or more.

What happens if the disease is not treated?

There is no known cure for AIDS. Most people who carry the HIV virus look and feel healthy, since it may take as long as 10 years before a person with HIV develops AIDS. Although medical science can prolong the lives of persons with AIDS, AIDS is almost always fatal.

How common is HIV/AIDS?

More than 1 million people are infected in the United States, and approximately 40,000 new people are infected each year.

Gonorrhea

What are the symptoms? (All people may not notice all symptoms.)

Pain or itching when urinating; frequent, urgent need to urinate; white or yellow discharge from penis or vagina; sore penis or vulva; sore throat.

Most women and some men have no early symptoms. Their only hope is that their sex partners will tell them they may have been infected.

How soon do the first symptoms appear?

Two to seven days after exposure. Early symptoms last about two to three weeks.

What happens if the disease is not treated?

Men: The germs spread through the body. If untreated, they can cause any or all of these problems: abscess in prostate gland; swollen, painful testicles; sterility; kidney damage.

Women: The infection usually centers in the cervix, spreading to all other sexual organs and may cause painful abscesses that leave scar tissue. The scar tissue often blocks fallopian tubes, making pregnancy impossible or very dangerous.

Both men and women may get acute arthritis and eye infections.

How common is gonorrhea?

Gonorrhea is a very common sexually transmitted disease. More than 700,000 people are infected each year.

Syphilis
What are the symptoms? (All people may not notice all symptoms.)

Stage 1: A sore (usually painless) on the penis, vulva, around the rectum, in the mouth, or on the lips. The sore is at the spot where the infection entered the body.

Stage 2: A rash (sometimes very faint) that may turn into sores in warm, wet areas; temporary hair loss; swollen glands.

How soon do the first symptoms appear?

Stage 1: Ten to 90 days or more after exposure. If left alone, the sore will go away within six weeks.

Stage 2: Three weeks to three months after the sore goes away. Without treatment, these symptoms go away within a few weeks or months.

What happens if the disease is not treated?

The patient's syphilis will remain hidden for months or years. Only a blood test can detect it. After anywhere from 2 to 40 years have passed, the following symptoms may occur: large destructive sores; heart problems; paralysis; insanity; irreparable damage to the baby during pregnancy.

How common is syphilis?

Roughly 32,000 cases of syphilis were reported in 2002.

Chlamydia

What are the symptoms? (All people may not notice all symptoms.)

Approximately 60 to 80 percent of women and 50 percent of men with chlamydia have no early symptoms. Symptoms, when they appear, are similar to gonorrhea (see above). Chlamydia germs can live in the body for years without causing noticeable symptoms. Faithful married couples are often shocked to learn that they both have chlamydia, caused by a sexual episode in one partner's past.

How soon do the first symptoms appear?

Usually three weeks after infection.

What happens if the disease is not treated?

Men: Inflamed urethra and testicles; possible inflammation of rectum; if untreated, sterility.

Women: Infected urethra and cervix. It may cause infertility, pregnancy in the fallopian tube, or inflammation of the pelvis. It's possible to infect newborn babies.

How common is chlamydia?

Nearly 3 million people are infected in the United States each year.

Genital Herpes

What are the symptoms? (All people may not notice all symptoms.)

Blisters or small bumps on penis and urethra or cervix, vagina, and vulva that may break and form open painful sores. Often the blisters are so small the person does not realize he or she has the disease and can pass it on to others. There may be pain when urinating. With the first infection, there may also be fever, joint pain, flu-like symptoms, itching, and tingling.

How soon do the first symptoms appear?

They appear 2–20 days after exposure. They may go away and reappear months later, even if there has been no sexual contact in between.

What happens if the disease is not treated?

May cause birth defects or death for a baby whose mother has herpes. There is strong evidence of a link between genital herpes and cancer of the cervix. Yearly Pap tests are advisable for women.

How common is genital herpes?

About 45 million people ages 12 and over have had a genital herpes infection, or about one in five people.

Human Papilloma Virus (HPV) (Genital Warts)

What are the symptoms? (All people may not notice all symptoms.)

Warts on the genital organs, from the size of a small tick to the size of a cauliflower.

How soon do the first symptoms appear?

Varies from a few weeks to years.

What happens if the disease is not treated?

The HPV virus may cause cancers of the cervix, vagina, vulva, and penis.

How common is HPV?

The Centers for Disease Control reports that 6.2 million Americans are infected with HPV each year and the total infected is 20 million. It is estimated that 50 percent of sexually active people will be infected with HPV. That number jumps to 80 percent for women over age 50.

Trichomoniasis

What are the symptoms? (All people may not notice all symptoms.)

Women: Yellowish-green smelly discharge; pain in pelvic area; soreness or severe itching in vulva.

Men: Most have no symptoms. Thin, whitish discharge, especially in the morning; tingling, itching sensation in penis.

How soon do the first symptoms appear?

They appear 5–28 days after exposure.

What happens if the disease is not treated?

The tiny parasites that cause "trich" will probably continue to multiply and cause discomfort. There is a link between trichomoniasis and cervical cancer.

How common is trichomoniasis?

More than 7.4 million new cases occur each year in women and men.

Other Questions

How can a person tell if she has an STD?

An examination by a doctor is the only way to find out for sure. If you notice any of the symptoms, see a doctor as soon as possible. An STD is easier to stop if it is diagnosed early and correctly. Do not try to treat yourself with antibiotics or other medicines. Each disease requires a different treatment.

There are other possible causes for most of the symptoms. For instance, pain during urination may be caused by a kidney or bladder infection. A discharge from the vagina could be perfectly normal or it could be a yeast infection (not an STD). If you are in doubt, see a doctor. Knowing for sure that you do not have an STD is important for your peace of mind.

Are you immune to an STD after you have had it?

No. The same person can get it again and again.

How likely am I to get an STD?

If you use your sexuality responsibly and wisely, you have very little chance of becoming infected. It's important, however, to inform yourself about STDs because

- you may need to advise and counsel friends who are less informed;

- it is possible—though unlikely—for a person who is not sexually active to get an STD;

- an untreated STD could destroy not only your life but the lives of your spouse and your baby.

Where can I go for help?

Here are some possibilities:

- *Your parents.* Most parents are loving, supportive, and forgiving when their teenagers come to them with major problems.

- *Your family doctor.* Level with the doctor. Without information only you can give, he or she may not suggest an STD as the possible cause of your symptoms.

- *A trusted school nurse or school counselor.* They will know where you can go for diagnosis and treatment.

- *Your pastor, a teacher, youth counselor, or some other trusted adult at your church.* Caring about your physical as well as spiritual health, this individual can guide and help you.

- *Your local public health clinic.* Look under your city or county name in the phone book. A public clinic is sometimes crowded and impersonal, but you are likely to find caring and competent people there. Public health doctors see so many STD cases that they become experts in their treatment. There will probably be no charge. If you are a minor, be sure to seek your parents' advice and help prior to taking action.

Oral and Anal Sex

Myth 7: *Are oral sex and anal sex really sex?*

Oral sex is a term used to identify either **fellatio**, applying the mouth or tongue to stimulate the penis, or **cunnilingus**, using the mouth or tongue to stimulate the vulva. Anal sex refers to the act whereby a male has intercourse with either a woman or another man by placing his penis into the other person's **anus**.

Both oral sex and anal sex have grown more common among young people in recent years. Many teens seem to consider this a so-called technical virginity and ignore the consequences of such acts, including a higher risk for some sexually-transmitted diseases. Although both of these activities avoid the risk of pregnancy, they are in fact sex acts. Those in dating relationships do well to avoid these and all other sex acts that go against God's natural reproductive design.

Cohabitation

Myth 8: *Is living together outside of marriage really all that bad? Plenty of people seem to be doing it.*

Living together outside of marriage clearly offends God's will regarding sexual purity. God's will for a happy and fulfilling life makes no room for sexual relationships outside of those reserved for a husband and wife within marriage. Living together, or *cohabitation*, disregards the commitment to one another that God designed for the institution of marriage. Fornication (sexual relationships outside of marriage) dishonors both God the Creator and the men and women who freely take part in it.

The argument that living together gives a man and woman the opportunity to test out whether they would be compatible in marriage has been shown to be scientifically unsupported. Research has shown statistically that couples who live together prior to marriage are more likely to divorce than those who do not.

Cohabitation harms relationships in the following ways:

• People who cohabit prior to marriage exhibit a greater difficulty with solving problems than those who don't.

• Cohabiting leads to more individualistic attitudes and behaviors, which work against a healthy marriage where two people must submit to one another in love.

• Cohabiting actually convinces young people that relationships are fragile and temporary, thus making them more accepting of the idea of divorce.

• Domestic violence is higher in cohabiting relationships than among married couples.

• Cohabitants experience more drunkenness and depression than married couples.

• People in cohabiting relationships are more likely to be unfaithful to their partners than married couples.

Contrary to what the culture would have you believe, research shows that the benefits of God's design for marriage cannot be replaced by sinful and self-serving relationships.

Virginity

Myth 9: *Can virginity be restored once it has been lost through sexual activity?*

God's plan is for men and women to reserve acts of sexual intimacy for their spouse. Once men or women have taken part in sexual activities reserved for marriage, they have lost their virginity whether or not they are married.

Some people stay virgins until they are married but are filled with impure thoughts and desires. Others may have lost their virginity but have repented and work to live out their calling to have a pure heart. God wants our thoughts, desires, and behaviors to be pure, but none of us has lived that perfectly. Just about everyone has disobeyed God's will with regard to sexuality. Impure sexual thoughts as well as sinful attitudes and actions all fall under God's judgment and condemnation. Thank God He has sent His Son to earn forgiveness for all sins, including those involving our sexuality.

Through the power of His Holy Spirit, God has given us the desire and ability to begin again as new people, forgiven and holy in the sight of God and eager to live for Him. Second Corinthians 5:14–15 reminds us, "For the love of Christ controls us, because we have concluded this: that one has died for all, therefore all have died; and He died for all, that those who live might no longer live for themselves but for Him who for their sake died and was raised" (ESV).

Chapter 4

The Challenges of Becoming a Woman

Have you ever stopped to think what it means to be a young woman in today's culture? It's an important question—so important, in fact, that much of your life will depend on how you answer it.

Our culture has its own ideas of what it means to be a woman. If you watch popular TV shows, being a woman means being glamorous and sexy. If you listen to popular music, being a woman often means going to bed with a lot of men—but making no commitments to any of them. If you read women's magazines, you might think a real woman is all about spending money for fashions, shoes, and beauty products.

Growing up, you may have asked yourself if these portrayals of women are realistic or healthy. Yet chances are you have tried to meet these stereotypes at times. It's difficult to swim against the tide of popular culture. It seems like everyone wants to live a glamorous life.

In the past, the path to womanhood was fairly clear. Young girls watched and helped their mothers work at home, cooking and cleaning. Dating as we now know it was virtually nonexistent; parents arranged marriages between young people based on family backgrounds and ability to produce a large family. When a girl began to take enough responsibility on her own, she was considered a woman.

We may look back and be glad we didn't live in earlier times. Certainly life in the past was full of hardship and difficulties. There are still hardships and difficulties for young women today.

Take a moment to examine the influence of pop culture on your perceptions of sexuality and what it means to be a young woman.

Sexuality in the Media

Consider the influence of popular media. How many TV programs show strong, loving parents who take an active interest in their children? How many movies show faithful husbands and wives who don't sleep around or single people who aren't interested in just having sex with as many people as possible? How does popular music treat the topic of sexuality?

What attitudes about sex do you see reflected in

• the books or magazines you read or look at?

• the movie you saw most recently?

• your favorite TV show?

• the songs you listen to?

• the images you see on some Internet sites?

Do these show responsible, sexual persons, who, though imperfect and vulnerable, have a set of values? Or do they picture glamorous figures who live in a world of fantasy? Does the story tell of trust, communication, and caring between two loving people? Or does it imply that physical attraction is all that matters?

Many ads, movies, TV shows, and other media seem to be written for the lowest level of maturity and intelligence. If we constantly fill our minds with words and pictures that show sex as an aggressive and impersonal act, we may find it hard to maintain our own moral values and to develop lasting, loving relationships.

On the other hand, we can learn from movies, books, and other media that honestly describe a growing relationship between two real people, even if those people act in ways we might disagree with. We can learn from both the good and the bad choices of others.

Even when a book or a movie appears to reflect real life with reasonable honesty, you may wonder whether things would really turn out the way they do in the story. Here's a plot you may have seen recently: Shortly after the hero and heroine meet and fall in love, they hop into bed. There are no doubts, no second thoughts, and no worries about unwelcome consequences. Sexual intercourse appears to be a normal, expected part of dating.

• What movies or TV shows have you seen that imply that sex outside of marriage is okay because everybody does it?

• What effect might this subtle message have on a person who has not thought through her own values?

• Have you ever heard the statement *sex sells*? Does it help to explain why bedroom scenes are found in so many books, TV shows, and movies? What about advertisements that imply that a given product will make you sexier or more attractive?

Now ask yourself an important question again, and answer it honestly: how much has the culture influenced how you understand sexuality?

You may think it hasn't influenced you very much. In fact, most young people don't think they personally are very affected by the media they consume. But most of them believe their friends are very influenced by pop culture. Studies show that even young adults into their mid-twenties are significantly impacted by the sex shown on TV.

If our ideas about sex can be so influenced by popular culture, perhaps our understanding of what it means to be a woman can be similarly influenced.

Don't think so? It is now becoming common among young people to serial date—that is, to move from one boyfriend to another with no real objective for long-term commitment or marriage. Even Christian young adults often delay marriage endlessly in order to play longer. Is that your goal, to play when you grow up? Sadly, many of these Christian young men who are not moving toward marriage are pressuring the young women they know to provide some of the benefits of marriage by acting out with them sexually apart from God's design.

You may be wondering, If this isn't what I am supposed to be doing, what is my life supposed to be like?

A Biblical Look

Let's go back to the beginning and review this book's lessons in light of your call to become a godly woman.

From the very beginning, it is clear that God made us for relationships with Him and with other people. Examine your life to see if you are in a strong relationship with God. If you feel distant from God or don't spend time in prayer, worship, and Bible reading, you may find yourself growing apart from God. Distancing yourself from God is also likely to affect your relationships with others.

At one time we were separated from God, but we have been brought back into relationship with Him through Jesus Christ, our Lord and Savior. Jesus is our bridge to healthy relationships with God and others. The first step in becoming a godly young woman is to allow Christ to be the center of your life. Lutheran theologian Dietrich Bonhoeffer said that we are never as close to another person as when we approach him or her through Christ.

The irony of living in a fallen world is that even though our deepest desire is to be close to God and others, sin so often ends up moving us farther apart. If this is true, embracing Christ daily is truly the first step in living out your calling as one of God's beloved children.

Looking back to our creation, another point becomes clear: In being made for others, we are called not to selfishness but to service. God calls men and women to serve one another, not to take advantage of one another. Remember the words of Ephesians 5. Both spouses are called to submit to one another. This is because service is at the heart of God's love for us.

Reading the Gospels, we can see that Jesus' chief characteristic was love demonstrated by service to God and to others. True love gives itself to others; it does not take from them. It seems that many cultural messages have twisted this eternal truth. Being a strong woman has been distorted so that many view it as being in a position to control or dominate others. Was this what Jesus did?

On the contrary, He gave Himself for others, even to the point of death on a cross. As a child of God, your daily living out of this calling leads you to give to others in many self-sacrificing ways. Consider simply treating others with common courtesy. Opening a door to allow others to go before you requires putting yourself last. Managing employees at work involves serving them and making sure they have what they need to get their jobs done.

How does this play out in intimate relationships? You may have strong sexual desires for your boyfriend, but serving him in love requires that you put those desires aside until marriage. In such cases, you together decide to value decency and godliness above your own desires. Many people do not act this way, unfortunately, and end up bringing self-serving attitudes into marriage with them.

Do you imagine that once you get married you can then have everything you want? Serving your spouse in marriage means that you continue that same self-giving love. True godly love involves each of you giving yourself to the other. Because of sin, you may have to struggle to keep from viewing your spouse as someone who should give you whatever you ask or desire.

Another important lesson in becoming a godly woman is repentance. God demands perfection from us, but we can't deliver it. He gave us His own Son to be perfect in our stead. Throughout the Bible, we are called to be repentant of our sins. A godly woman is not a perfect woman but one who quickly admits and apologizes for her mistakes.

Perhaps you have not been pure with a boy in the past—or even now. Are you sorry? Have you stopped going against God's calling? If you are not sorry or have not apologized to God, you are in rebellion against God. Maybe you have tried to stop but keep falling back into your sin and are worried God won't forgive you. You may think:

How can I go back and ask for forgiveness again? I keep doing the same thing over and over. It's hopeless.

Remember the story of the prodigal son (Luke 15:11–32)? The runaway boy was just as ashamed of himself as you are. The sensible thing for his dad to do would have been to take him back on probation: You can come home if you shape up. But the father ran to meet him, put a ring on his finger, and gave him a party! That's the way your Father in heaven feels about you.

Even if it's the 27th time I've come home?

That's right. God's love for you does not depend on good behavior, for "While we were still sinners, Christ died for us" (Romans 5:8).

I can't believe that God approves of my behavior.

You are right. He loves you always—that's why He may not approve of all your behavior. He wants you to grow more loving in what you do.

But how can I change? I've tried and tried, but it doesn't do any good!

Daily invite His Spirit to live in you and work through you. If you fail sometimes, keep coming back for more forgiveness. Remember, even St. Paul complained that "What I do is not the good I want to do; no, the evil I do not want to do—this I keep on doing" (Romans 7:19). So there is a power inside us, leading us to sin. But we have God's own power too. "That power is like the working of His mighty strength, which He exerted in Christ when He raised Him from the dead" (Ephesians 1:19–20). Stop trying so hard, and yield yourself to the fantastic power God gives you as His forgiven child.

Admitting that you have failed or sinned against someone takes a great deal of courage and much humility. In fact, maturing into a godly woman requires that you develop a humble spirit. All the world seems calculated to appeal to our pride and vanity. TV reality shows feature participants who will do anything for their 15 minutes of fame. The truly humble woman is a rarity, but she stands out all the more because it is so difficult.

Do you remember the parable of the two men in the temple praying to God? (See Luke 18:9–14.) The Pharisee was at the front of the temple, thanking God he wasn't like all the sinners out there. The other man was too ashamed to go to the front. He stood in the back with his head hung low, asking God to be merciful because he was a sinner. Jesus tells us that the second man went home justified before God. God desires humility in us. If we serve God humbly, who else need we impress?

Becoming a godly woman is not easy. The world of sin is appealing at times and very insistent that we stray from God's plan. You can succeed, however, by placing Christ at the center of your life, learning from and following His example of service in love, repenting when you fail, and keeping a humble spirit. Keep these qualities in mind as you read the following chapters dealing more specifically with navigating relationships.

Jesus Demonstrated God's Love

Above all, remember that your true identity cannot be found in a boyfriend or in worldly things but only in Christ alone. Through Jesus, we have been adopted into God's own family forever.

One of Jesus' jobs here on earth was to demonstrate to you that God loves you in a very personal way. A leper, Levi the tax collector, a widow, Simon the Pharisee, a prostitute—Jesus made each of them feel important and loved.

How many teachers today would bother having class if there were a big snowstorm and only one student was there? Not many. Yet if you page through the Gospel of Luke, you'll notice that Jesus spent a lot of His time teaching or healing just one person.

When you share feelings or problems with God, remember that you are very special in His sight. Incredible though it seems, you have His undivided attention. You don't have to do anything or be anything to get Him to love you. He just does—and He always will. He "did not spare His own Son, but gave Him up for us all—how will He not also, along with Him, graciously give us all things" (Romans 8:32)?

Chapter 5

Dating

Now that you've thought about what God's plan for sexuality is and how to grow into a godly woman, how can you apply this knowledge toward a dating relationship? Have you ever asked any of the following questions?

Does a person have to date to be considered normal?

How does one get started dating?

Is dating only one person a good idea?

What is the best way to handle a breakup?

How much physical contact is okay?

What if we've already had intercourse?

Questions, questions. There sure are a lot of them when it comes to dating.

Help from the Bible

Does the Bible talk about dating?

Not exactly. In Bible times, parents usually arranged for the marriage of their children, just as Abraham did for his son Isaac to Rebekah. Like Christian parents today, parents in Bible times who knew and trusted in the one true God were concerned that their children found a believing spouse.

Traditionally, dating in western societies is regarded as an activity in which individuals of the opposite sex spend time together. Ultimately they may recognize that they get along well together and desire to build a common future in marriage. God's Word has much to say about human sexuality and the corresponding types of thoughts, words, and actions appropriate and healthy for God's children, whether they are married or single.

Why don't you do some reading in God's Word, check it out for yourself? You'll be sure to find examples, insights, and guidelines that will help you make good decisions.

I don't like being preached at, though.

Who does? But that doesn't make God's Law any less true. "The wages of sin"—including sexual sin—"is death" (Romans 6:23). God's Word is very clear about that. The Bible is pretty specific in labeling sexual sins and warning Christians about them. For example, "God will judge the adulterer and all the sexually immoral" (Hebrews 13:4). Or, "Flee from sexual immorality. All other sins a man commits are outside his body, but he who sins sexually sins against his own body" (1 Corinthians 6:18).

The great thing, though, is that God doesn't just give us warnings. He stands at our side to *help* us. Notice, for example, how that Corinthians passage goes on: "Do you not know that your body is a temple of the Holy Spirit, who is in you, whom you have received from God? You are not your own; you were bought at a price. Therefore honor God with your body" (1 Corinthians 6:19–20).

What does that mean, "You were bought at a price"?

St. Peter put it this way: "For you know that it was not with perishable things such as silver or gold that you were redeemed . . . but with the precious blood of Christ" (1 Peter 1:18–19). Jesus loved us enough to die for us! That's what our Christian faith is all about.

It does help me to remember that Jesus loved me that much! And that He gives me His Holy Spirit.

It puts a new light, too, on the false value that says, "Try not to hurt anyone, but if it feels good, do it!"

Yes, that kind of lifestyle ignores who I am—as a Christian, I mean.

It sure does. You are more than a body. St. Paul lays it on the line when he says: "Live a life of love, just as Christ loved us and gave Himself up for us. . . . Among you there must not be even a hint of sexual immorality, or of any kind of impurity, . . . because these are improper for God's holy people" (Ephesians 5:2–8).

That's a lot to live up to.

It's a way—the only way—to be really free. We don't have to do "what everyone else is doing." We're able to say either yes or no—remembering who we are as God's own people and counting on His forgiveness when we fail.

Great! But could we get to some of those specific questions about dating now?

Yes, but before we do, consider this: Most dating situations you have questions about will give you an opportunity either to develop more into a godly young woman who serves others or to grow further away from this ideal. Your goal should be to develop into the kind of person that young men will want to be with and eventually marry. Too often we are focused on what the other person can do for us. Chances are, young Christian men are looking for mature, kind, thoughtful, loving young women who value and respect them without trying to take advantage of them. Does this describe you? If not, get working!

Wanting to Be Popular
What can I do so other kids will like me?

Many psychologists have conducted experiments that try to find out the reasons why some people have more friends than others.

They discovered that the most popular people are those who like others and are pleased when others like them. Yet they are not terribly worried if someone doesn't like them. (Interesting, isn't it, how this relates to what God intends for us: that we grow as *loving persons!*) The more relaxed you are, the better you will do in a social situation. Don't allow yourself to worry and fret about what people will think of you. *Expect* them to like you. Why shouldn't they? Concentrate instead on getting to know *them*.

The researchers also found that people make friends with those they see often in pleasant circumstances. You're not going to meet many people while you are in your room at home.

It's nice to be popular. There are times, though, when the price is too high. Sometimes it's necessary to choose between doing the right thing and being liked by the group you are in at the time. Often the choice is easier than it looks. The first person to speak up and say, "I don't think this is a good idea" may be surprised by the number of others who have been thinking the same thing.

My mom and dad are always criticizing what I wear. They say it's too provocative. Don't they get it? That's the style today. Modesty is out. Don't I have a right to dress like the other kids in my class?

Let's look at this issue from three perspectives. Let's begin with you. Did you know that clothing is a language that speaks a message? What message are you giving about your own self-respect? Do you want people to notice you because of external factors, or do you want them to know the real you—who you are inside, as a person? How you respect yourself influences how others will respect you. Do you want people, especially boys, to treat you with dignity, decency, courtesy, and respect? Then you need to dress respectfully, with dignity, and with decency. This isn't a call to be prudish, old-fashioned, or frumpy. It is a call for moderation—within reasonable standards, not given to extremes. It takes courage to recognize and resist negative cultural and peer group influences in order to find Christian standards and an appropriate style for yourself. Look to God to make you strong: "Be strong and courageous. Do not be frightened, and do not be dismayed, for the LORD your God is with you wherever you go" (Joshua 1:9 ESV).

Second, let's look at this issue from the perspective of boys. It is tempting for a girl to dress in a revealing way, flaunting sexuality, in order to get noticed by boys. But a relationship based on being noticed as a sex object is troubled from the start. Young males are easily visually stimulated and become sexually aroused quickly. This does not excuse them from having lustful reactions. They are responsible for their own behavior. But as a Christian young woman, you need to give consideration to the impact of how you dress. Out of concern for others, you should not tempt them to do wrong, nor should you encourage them to act on their weaknesses. Once again, the Scriptures are a guide. As 1 Corinthians 10:23–24 states, in reference to believers not being bound by the Law, which Christ fulfilled: "'All things are lawful,' but not all things are helpful. 'All things are lawful,' but not all things build up. Let no one seek his own good, but the good of his neighbor" (ESV).

The third perspective considers the matter of God's will for our lives. Most young women desire to be pretty, popular, and loved. For that reason, Satan twists these ideas in our thinking so that we not only say "everybody does it," but we also say "I have a right to . . . , " which ends up translating into "I have a right to do whatever I want." This kind of thinking goes all the way back to Eden. Eve thought God limited her choices. She wanted to be her own god, setting her own rules; and we know what a catastrophe resulted! The clothes you wear may seem a simple personal choice by comparison. But that choice is not so simple—it is a reflection of what you value. How you dress can indicate what is most important to you. As we live in the presence of God each day, we are encouraged to remember that "whether you eat or drink or whatever you do, do it all for the glory of God" (1 Corinthians 10:31). Remember that your value comes from being a loved child of God. You are so valuable to God that He gave up His only Son to save you and to make you His own!

Today's world is a hostile environment for Christians. More and more, we see that today's society is ready to accept anything, except God's will. It takes integrity and commitment on your part to make God-fearing choices, as you are led by the Holy Spirit. Again the Bible leads us not to conform to the world but to be transformed (changed, made unique, dedicated). Romans 12:1–2 says, "I urge you . . . in view of God's mercy, to offer your bodies . . . holy and pleasing to God . . . Do not conform any longer to the pattern of this world, but be transformed by the renewing of your mind." God's way is not the easy way; it takes courage. But God calls on us to be strong, even as young people, as we see in 1 Timothy 4:12, "Don't let anyone look down on you because you are young, but set an example for the believers in speech, in life, in love, in faith and in purity."

Getting a Date

I've been saying "Hi" all semester to a boy in my English class, but that's as far as it goes. How can I get to know him better?

Greeting someone with a big smile is a good start. Some days, try to leave class at the same time he does. Ask him a question about the homework assignment; tell him what you heard about the next test; joke with him. You might gradually become better friends; then, one of you might suggest doing something together—maybe as a part of a larger group.

It could be, though, that as you get to know each other, you'll find you really don't have much in common. That's why it's smarter not to pin all your hopes on one person. Your best bet is to make friends with many people.

It took me weeks to work up courage enough to talk to Matthew after class. He just said, "I gotta go," and left. What's wrong with me?

Why do you think something is wrong with you? If he acted nervous, maybe he was! Speak to him in a group situation where he might feel more comfortable. If he still seems unfriendly, forget him and move on.

Everybody is rejected at one time or another. (That's why it's so great to know that God keeps on loving us in Christ!) If you think of something you said or did that may have cooled his interest in you, learn from that. Don't worry about it—his disinterest was most likely caused by his interest in someone else (simply a matter of timing) or by some other problem in his life.

Value yourself. Remember that you're God's own person. Although it may seem impossible at the time, you will find other boys who do appreciate you.

After six weeks of talking to Jake after history class, he finally asked me out. It was a disaster—neither of us had a good time. What went wrong?

You probably didn't have very much in common. Next time, get to know someone you feel comfortable with, a boy who seems to enjoy your company. If you don't know any boys that well, look for a group of guys and girls who do things together. Some people are active members of two groups at church because the groups have so many social activities.

Is there anything wrong with going out on a blind date?

Many successful marriages began with the introduction of a man and a woman by a person or couple known to both of them. Usually, however, people find it more comfortable to get to know someone in the company of mutual friends before spending time alone together on a date.

What about a pickup date?

Warnings against "being picked up" or "hooking up" with someone you just met are the teenage and adult equivalent of warning young children not to go with strangers. The consequences can be just as traumatic. Though you may think you are a good judge of character, and though the other person may appear "cool" or "cute," first impressions often are incorrect, leading to situations where there might be physical, mental, emotional, or spiritual danger and harm.

Obviously, going with a boy you don't know for the purpose of sexual activity disobeys God's Law, just as it shows disrespect for the other person and for yourself. People who are willing to "pick up" or to be picked up want instant satisfaction. They seek "fun" on a one-night-stand basis, but it can be very dangerous, even life-threatening. God's Word is clear that you are called to give yourself in love. Engaging in a brief sexual encounter with a virtual stranger is about as far from God's example of love as you can get.

Dating More Than One Person

I know that Paul (whom I like fairly well) would like me to go to the prom with him. I would rather go with David (whom I like very much). But if I say no to Paul and David doesn't ask me, I won't get to go at all. What should I do?

How would you feel if you were Paul and were kept waiting while other options were explored? How would you feel if the situation was reversed and you were the one "left dangling" while someone searched for another date? Are you going to handle this situation in a self-serving way or with kindness?

Is it a good idea to tell a boy you like him a lot? I've only gone out with Nathan twice, but he already means more to me than any other boy ever has. My friends tell me to play hard to get, but that seems so dishonest.

Playing games with people's feelings *is* dishonest. It's silly to pretend to be standoffish unless you really feel that way.

However, you can choose one of several ways to let Nathan know you like him a lot. You can push for a steady relationship he's not ready for. If you do, he may be embarrassed and irritated and might drop you.

Another choice made by many people is to express their feelings by encouraging sexual intimacy. That's even more dishonest; it's pretending to have the deeply committed permanent relationship people have in marriage. Pretending won't make it true. Most of all, such sexual intimacy is wrong because it leaves God out of the relationship.

(Remember all those specific Bible texts we looked at in the beginning of this chapter.)

The best way to let Nathan know how you feel about him is to appreciate him. Tell him the strengths and talents you have seen in him. Notice the thoughtful things he does for you. Be kind and considerate of his feelings. Most people like someone who is kind to them and appreciates them.

Is there something wrong with me because I don't want to date?

Many young people do little or no dating during their teen years. These non-daters usually have friends of both sexes, and they spend time with their friends.

The group gets together for parties, basketball games—whatever. Sometimes closer friendships form within the group—people find others they can talk to, confide in.

The most interesting groups are very flexible about their membership. New people are welcome, and no one is pressured to participate in any one activity. Often one person will belong to several informal groups. It's a no-hassle way to become more comfortable with people of the other sex.

A boy I've gone out with a couple times asked me to a pool party. I wear a brace on one leg. After I remove the brace, I can swim fairly well, but my leg is thin and funny-looking. Will my handicap make a difference to him?

It depends on the boy. Some boys would admire you for dealing with your handicap. Others might be embarrassed and uncomfortable (which is their problem, not yours). The safest plan might be to tell him about your leg now, so he has time to get used to the idea. Be matter-of-fact, not apologetic. If you have a positive attitude about yourself, chances are others will also. If he doesn't react well, he is showing a character flaw, and you are probably better off without him.

My father won't let me go to a boy's house when his parents aren't home. When a boy comes to our house, we're not left alone for more than a few minutes. Why doesn't my father trust me?

Maybe he trusts your integrity and your dependability but is a little uneasy about your judgment. Being alone with a person you like can be very exciting. It's tempting to let things go further than you intended.

That doesn't mean that your body will take over and you will be unable to stop yourself. It is always possible to stop, but it may be very difficult. Your father may see this less as a matter of not trusting you and more as a matter of not trusting your date. He is probably concerned most about protecting you and your reputation.

Why should I have to watch out for my reputation just because I'm a female? My mother keeps nagging me that my clothes and makeup might give people the wrong idea about me. My parents seem comfortable letting my brother do whatever he wants because he's a male. It doesn't seem fair!

I can appreciate how you feel, but the Bible doesn't make any moral distinction between men and women when it calls Christians to be lights in a dark world. How else will people come to know about Jesus, except from Jesus' people? And how interested will they be in what we have to say if we have a bad reputation? God holds males and females equally responsible and accountable for their thoughts, attitudes, and actions.

I didn't intend to go out only with Jeff, but everyone assumes we are a couple. We've gone out three weekends in a row. I don't want to hurt him, but I don't like this trapped feeling. How do I get out?

Take the risk of sharing your feelings with Jeff. Be sure to make it clear that you really do enjoy his company. Maybe Jeff has been feeling trapped too. You might be able to work out an arrangement that permits you to see each other without either person feeling tied down.

It's good to get to know a lot of different young men. Why? You'll find out which qualities are important to you in a man. When the time comes that you are ready to marry, you will choose more wisely.

Dating Only One Person

My parents are furious because I exchanged rings with my boyfriend. In my high school, you either go out with only one person or you don't date at all, but my parents can't seem to understand this. How can I get them to see my side?

Most people see one person for a few months, then another and another. If you see your relationship as one that is probably temporary, your parents won't worry quite as much.

Explain to your parents that dating only one person makes it easier to get together casually. As you do ordinary things together, you get to know each other very well. Managing this relationship can be good practice for marriage someday.

Of course, they're probably afraid you may "practice for marriage" in other ways. They have no way of knowing what you're thinking if you don't talk—and listen—to them. Let them see how responsible you are about keeping any agreement you make about things like hours, unsupervised time alone together, alcohol, and the places you go.

Right now my boyfriend and I (both 17 years old) think we want to spend the rest of our lives together. But we realize we'll both change a lot in the next few years. How can we keep from getting too serious too soon?

Each of you should have some activities in which you are independent of the other—different jobs, schools, clubs—anything that will help you learn to know yourselves as separate persons. Talk honestly and openly about what is happening in your relationship. Make individual plans for the future, but remind yourselves that joint plans must be tentative. Consciously turn your bodies over to Christ. Together, ask Him to help you guard against hurting each other with too much physical intimacy too soon.

I can't help being very jealous of my boyfriend. One day a note fell out of his pocket. I grabbed it and read it. It was from another girl! It was just about their history assignment, but I was furious! Shouldn't he stop exchanging notes with other girls when he's MY boyfriend?

Do the words "MY boyfriend" mean a close, caring relationship, or do they mean owning another person? Very few people are willing to have no life at all outside a relationship. Even in a marriage, most people do not read their spouse's mail unless invited to do so.

Grab hold of God's love for you in Jesus. He will help you feel less insecure. (See chapter 4 or talk to an older person you trust.)

I have been offered a summer job as drama coach at a camp about 150 miles from home. My boyfriend has a good job right here in town. If I go away, we might not see each other all summer. I need the money and the experience, but is it worth taking a chance on losing my boyfriend?

By the time fall comes, both of you will be more independent, more interesting persons. You'll have many new experiences and ideas to share. You could end up closer than ever.

Even if you stay at home, you are taking a chance that you will lose your boyfriend. People change, especially when they are young. It hurts when a friendship dies, but clinging to each other will make no difference.

If you truly have a strong relationship, it will not wither away because of a summer's separation.

I've been going with Michael for about four months, but lately he's been talking about maybe getting married someday. Even though I like Michael a lot, I'm not ready to even THINK about being serious. I don't want to lose him, and I don't want to hurt him. What can I do?

Be honest with Michael. Ask Jesus to help you speak your mind and heart. The conversation could be painful, but it's not fair to let Michael believe you see the future as he does.

But what will happen if you let things go on as they are? Steady dating at a young age often leads to a teenage marriage, especially when the couple feels committed to each other. Five or 10 years later, one or both partners may bitterly regret closing off their options at such a young age and want out. Of course many young marriages do succeed (often after a rough struggle). But statistics show that teenage marriages are three times as likely to fail as are marriages of people in their 20s. By shrinking from painful honesty now, you could store up a lot more pain for both of you—and for possible children—later.

I like a boy now but feel like maybe I should keep searching for my soul mate.

This may seem like a very romantic notion, but chances are God doesn't have just one person who is perfectly compatible with you. Many people search and search for that one right person and never find him. Others marry someone they think is their soul mate only to be disappointed after they become husband and wife. The truth is there is no one person who is perfectly right for any of us. None of us finds someone we are completely happy with—even when we look into the mirror. Such are the consequences of sin.

It is important for you to seek out a young man with godly characteristics who would make a good husband and father. Such a husband is already your soul mate because you share a oneness in Jesus your Savior and the new life you have in Him through Baptism. You will find a deep relationship that will extend into eternity as you plan prayerfully and build a life based on Christ's forgiveness and love. You will appreciate the virtues of your godly husband more and more as together you establish a marriage and family founded upon God and His Word.

Breaking Up

I have been upset ever since Andy broke up with me. I can't eat, can't sleep, can't study. All I do is sit around and think about him. Help!

The grief that you are feeling is a powerful emotion. You probably feel that you will never be truly happy again. Talk to Jesus about your feelings. Tell Him how it hurts. You may not feel any lightening of your mood, any real sense that He is there, but He is listening, and He does care, and it will make a difference.

Remember that Jesus often works through other people, including you. Find a trustworthy friend you can talk to about your feelings. If possible, establish a new, casually friendly relationship with Andy. When you find yourself thinking about him, remind yourself firmly that this painful time will pass, and do something else. This is a good time to get reacquainted with family, develop new interests, and make new friends.

When you do begin dating again, be cautious for a while. Your pride has been hurt. Don't rush into a new relationship; you may unconsciously be using the new person to prove you are still lovable.

Jon and I went steady for about two years. We thought we loved each other and sincerely intended to get married someday. After we broke up, I felt pretty guilty—even though we never had intercourse, we came close to it many times.

I've asked God to forgive me, and I know He has. But somehow I don't FEEL forgiven. Why do my guilty feelings keep coming back? Will I always feel guilty about Jon, even after I marry someone else?

It is unlikely that the guilt you feel now will be a problem years later in your marriage. If you realize you have faced your sin and have been forgiven, you are free to go on with the business of living.

However, you will probably always regret what happened between you and Jon. The love you two felt for each other was an honest, real emotion, a gift of God. But the way you expressed that emotion was both wrong and unwise.

It is foolish to assume that teenage love will last forever. Most people have so many new experiences during their teens that they almost certainly will change—in an unpredictable direction. The teenage relationship may last, but it may not.

Because you acted on the assumption that your feelings would not change, you hurt Jon and yourself. God's forgiveness does not instantly erase all consequences. Only time—and God—can heal the emotional damage that happens when people invest so much of themselves in a relationship that does not work out.

Intimacy

How far can I go and still respect myself and my boyfriend?

Before anyone will respect you, you must respect yourself. Instead of asking, How far can I go? Try, What is honest between us? What is best for us? What honors us as people who belong to God?

God wants only what is best for us. In His divine plan, He has reserved sexual intimacy for marriage. His plan is for those who are not married to remain *abstinent*, that is, to not engage in sexual intercourse and other acts of intimacy reserved for persons married to each other. God desires His people to be set apart—to not fall into the behavioral patterns associated with those who do not know and trust in Jesus as their Savior. "For the grace of God has appeared, bringing salvation for all people, training us to renounce ungodliness and worldly passions, and to live self-controlled, upright, and godly lives in the present age" (Titus 2:11–12 ESV).

How can I tell how much intimacy I can have with a boy?

Some people think that it is up to the girl to decide, so then the boy can follow the macho creed of "get all I can," while he depends on the girl to protect him from a relationship he's not emotionally ready for.

That's not only wrong, it's old-fashioned and immature. A good relationship is based on mutual respect and mutual responsibility. You have God's Word for your guide.

"You were bought at a price. Therefore honor God with your body" (1 Corinthians 6:20).

I love my boyfriend very much, and I know he loves me, but we're afraid of going out of control. What can we do?

Avoid unsupervised and unplanned situatons as well as alcohol. Instead, focus on your love and respect for your boyfriend and for your relationship.

Your mutual love for each other can make all the difference as can your mutual love for Jesus, who loves you both. When you truly care for someone, you are not likely to put your own temporary pleasure ahead of the long-term happiness of both persons. When you believe in Jesus, His will and His love for you enters into the relationship.

Remember that the farther you go along the road that leads to intercourse, the more difficult it is to put on the brakes and turn around. However, it is always possible to stop. You—and your faith in Jesus—are bigger than your feelings.

As has been mentioned already, these situations may seem very trying for you, but they are real opportunities to practice and cultivate the traits necessary to become a godly woman. By controlling yourself, you are letting the boy know that you are willing to serve, cherish, and respect him. This self-control may be one of your most attractive qualities to a young man who is also seeking to follow God's plan for his sexuality.

My boyfriend says he loves me more than I love him because he's ready for intercourse and I'm not. I'm afraid I will lose him if I don't do what he wants.

You might try talking with him about your relationship with Jesus and how important His love and His will are in your life—your earthly life as well as your eternal one. If your boyfriend is a Christian, you may be able to explore together what God's Word says about *fornication*— intercourse outside of marriage—and about the beauty of sexual intercourse within the marriage relationship. (See chapter 7.)

If your boyfriend is not a Christian and remains insistent, ask yourself: What kind of love for you, really, does he have if it requires you to damage your relationship with Christ in order to satisfy his physical desires? Is it lust masquerading as love? Do you want to encourage a continuing pattern where he uses pressure to get whatever he wants? If he's threatening to dump you unless you do what he wants, is this the kind of love you can build a future on?

How can I get the willpower to say, "this far and no farther," and stick to it? I feel so guilty sometimes, even though I have never had intercourse.

You need to talk to God about those guilt feelings. Remember, there is no sin so terrible that you cannot ask for—and receive—His forgiveness. He will never, for any reason, stop loving you.

Whatever you've been doing that you feel guilty about, don't do it! Of course that isn't as easy as it sounds, especially when willpower is something you feel you lack. You probably have the will but not the power.

The good news is that the power doesn't have to come from you. The power comes from Christ who died for you and rose again. He lives in you. The closer you are to Him, the more power you will have. So read your Bible, pray, and commune with Him in His Supper. As you get ready to go out on a date, ask Him to be with you, and trust in *His* power, not your own.

The power He gives you is not a matter of gritting your teeth and being too serious. When things get intense on a date, often a little humor will relieve the tension. Or you can explain to your date, quite seriously, that you care too much about him to let anything happen you'd both regret.

The other thing to remember is that it takes time—and usually some mistakes—to fully develop a strong sense of self-control. That's why this book uses the term *cultivate* when discussing how to build up godly qualities. The results don't appear overnight; they take time and constant weeding, watering, and nourishing with prayer and Bible study. Growing up in Christ is a daily process that extends over seasons of time. Having a goal to work toward is great, but realize that you have to practice before you will meet it consistently.

Chapter 6

Finding Out If
Love Is Real

As by God's grace you grow in your understanding of God's will for your sexuality and femininity, you may find yourself in more serious relationships. You may be wondering how your faith in Jesus and desire to live your life for Him applies to the practical question of whether you have a love that will last a lifetime.

What is the difference between infatuation and real love?

How can we tell if our love will last?

What qualities am I looking for in a mate?

What qualities are important to have in common with the one I will marry?

What does it mean if we fight?

Will marriage change us?

Will It Last?

Sixteen-year-old Josie is deeply in love with Brett, and Brett feels the same way about Josie. They live for the times when they are together. They have a world of their own. They feel intense excitement and pleasure each time they touch or even see each other. Is their love only infatuation—"puppy love"? No. It is real and genuine. When they promise to love each other always, they both really mean it.

Will their love last? It might. And then again, it might not. At this point in their lives, there's no way to tell. Between the ages of 15 and 21, most people change interests, attitudes, and some values. They discover new talents within themselves. They observe the way others live their lives and make some decisions about the shape their own lives will take.

Chances are, Josie and Brett will fall in love quite a few more times before they make a final choice of a mate. Each time they will learn more about how to love, how to have a satisfying relationship with another person. They will reevaluate what is important to them. These are times to consciously ask what the will of God is for them and what part He plays in their relationship. Keeping God central will improve their feelings about each other and their understanding of what it means to be male and female.

If love is based mainly on physical attraction, it may not last long. Without mutual liking and respect to keep it alive, sexual attraction withers away.

If you are wondering whether your love is a temporary one, notice the ways in which the relationship has changed you. If people say you have changed—and not for the better—look out! But if you are kinder, more responsible, more self-confident than you were before, you've got a good thing going, at least for this stage in your life. Remember that "in all things God works for the good of those who love Him" (Romans 8:28). God often uses a good relationship with another person to bring out the best in those He loves.

What to Look for in Someone to Love

Think about how you shop for important things like a car or a good stereo system. Chances are, you put a lot of thought into your purchase. You research quality and price and look for the best deal. In the end, you feel good about your purchase because of the time and effort you invested in it.

Shopping sounds like a cold-blooded term to apply to a human relationship. However, it's not a bad description of a good way to prepare for marriage.

Why is it that many people put so much effort into buying something expensive but don't invest the same time—or even more—into finding a potential marriage partner? Are you identifying the qualities necessary for someone to be a good husband and father, or will you wait to see who you happen to bump into at school or work?

Thinking deeply and praying about who you would match up well with is a good step toward finding that person. Then, as you get to know different people, you will discover which character traits are really important to you and the kinds of people with whom you feel most comfortable and happy. You also will pinpoint the qualities you absolutely could not stand in a life partner.

Character List for Lovers

Here is a list of qualities some people think are important in a mate. Which ones are absolutely essential? Which would you consider desirable extras? Which are you indifferent about?

able to handle disappointments without bitterness
able to see the funny side of things
adventurous
affectionate
ambitious
assertive
athletic
attractive
believes in God
can manage money
cares about other people
considerate
dependable
enthusiastic
even-tempered
forgiving
friendly
generous
gentle
good listener
good self-image
good talker
hard worker
independent thinker
intelligent

lives his faith
loves parties
neat
not a quitter
open-minded
patient
popular
quiet
rich
sense of humor
sensitive, understanding
sexually desirable
shares my main interests
well-dressed

Now look at the list in a different way. The key qualities you have identified are also likely to be important to the man you might want to marry. What will you have to offer? Do you live your faith? Are you someone who is dependable, someone whose word can be trusted? Are you able to laugh at yourself, able to see the funny side of life? Do you make an effort to be considerate, to treat people as you would like to be treated? Do you try to see things from the other person's point of view? As was mentioned in the last chapter, focusing on developing good qualities in yourself is at least as important as finding a potential mate with these qualities.

Don't be discouraged if you do not measure up to the expectations you yourself have for a marriage partner. Work at improving your weak spots. Building on the strengths you already have, you can become a person who has many positive qualities to bring to a marriage. You can become the person God intends you to be.

Giving yourself enough time and letting yourself become a little more mature will be helpful. It's good to remember, though, that age is no guarantee that people will make wise choices in love. Songs and literature often tell of mature people who made foolish choices. How then can a couple tell whether or not their love will last a lifetime? Here are some love signs you can watch for, some ways to test the durability of your love.

What Do We Have in Common?

The problem with our character list is that the same words mean different things to different people. Most of us would say we want an intelligent mate. But what we probably mean is that we'd like someone who is about as intelligent as we are, someone who has had about the same amount of education. When two people of unequal intelligence try to discuss anything, they both may feel bored and frustrated.

The same thing is true of many other words on the list. To one person, *adventurous* might mean a willingness to try a new restaurant (provided a friend recommends the place). To another person, *adventurous* might mean a spur-of-the-moment decision to move to Montana with no job, no money, and three children. There's nothing wrong with either of those attitudes, but those two people surely will have things to work through if they marry.

Often couples are attracted to each other by their differences. If you are a quiet, shy person, you might enjoy going out with a "life of the party" type to help overcome your shyness. Be cautious, though. What often happens is that the quiet one is dragged to parties by the social one, or the social one sits unhappily at home with the quiet one.

Another common difference is family background. What will happen if Lori and Jared fall in love? Jared's family life is lively, warm, and loud. Jared is the only one in his family who has graduated from high school. There isn't much money, but there's always an extra bed for a cousin from the country or a foster child who needs love.

In Lori's family, books and travel have always been important. Both of her parents have interesting, demanding careers. They are active in church and community affairs. Home is a quiet, restful place for relaxed conversation and listening to music.

Many couples as different as Jared and Lori have built happy marriages—and many have failed. Couples who are thinking of marriage should spend as much time as possible with each other's families. Differences may grow smaller as they get to know each other better. Or they may find the differences pose roadblocks to developing their love further. What one enjoys as a novelty doesn't always satisfy as a steady diet.

Will Marriage Change Us?

One of the things Julio loves about Maria is her enthusiasm. Whatever Maria does, she goes all out. Right now she's all wrapped up in dancing. Determined to be a professional dancer, she spends all her free time practicing—plus some time on homework and family responsibilities because her parents expect it.

"She'll settle down after we are married," Julio figures. "Of course she'll want to continue dancing, but she'll also want to work. Maria's love for me is stronger than her love for dancing."

Julio may be in for a surprise. It's unfair of him to attach unspoken conditions to his love for Maria. Although people can change, it's unrealistic to suppose that getting married will make it happen. Julio and Maria need to talk frankly about what each of them expects from marriage.

It's good that Maria has been open with Julio about the family conflicts caused by her intense desire to dance. Love often makes a person conceal some qualities or interests, lest they cause rejection by the loved one. That is both unwise and dishonest. It's important to set standards of appreciation, consideration, and unselfishness you are willing to live with for the rest of your life.

God's Holy Spirit enables Christians to grow in all the qualities that make a marriage a growing and happy relationship: "love, joy, peace, patience, kindness, goodness, faithfulness, gentleness and self-control" (Galatians 5:22–23).

Communication

In the best marriages, communication begins long before the couple heads for the church. Many hours need to be spent on the building of a friendship, talking about

> your faith in Christ;
> your complete life histories;
> your feelings about yourselves, your families;
> your interests, your sexuality, your goals.

Along with sharing life histories and future plans, communication involves active, loving listening to everyday problems and feelings.

Once a friendship is strong enough, each person develops the ability to listen without being defensive or trying to justify herself or himself. Healthy communication isn't a matter of who is right or wrong; it is effectively conveying thoughts, emotions, or feelings in a way that is mutually understood. Sometimes it's far more important to be loving than right.

Compassionate listening can be difficult for some. Keep in mind that men and women often look at things with a different perspective. Men tend to try to fix problems. If their wife or girlfriend comes to them with a problem, they offer suggestions or assistance to resolve it. Women don't think the same way, however. Often a woman simply wants to express her frustrations to someone who loves her. She doesn't necessarily want a solution; she wants affirmation.

Many women rank "good listener" as one of the most important qualities in a man. Women tend to be very verbal and want to know they are with someone who can hear what is important to them. Keep in mind that many partners might not be equally verbal, but they both can work at being a good listener.

What Happens When We Fight?

People who are in love still do have disagreements just like anybody else. Some couples are afraid to talk honestly. "If I tell her about that, she'll be angry." "If I tell him what I've decided to do, he'll try to stop me." Each tells the other only what he or she wants to hear. Each is very careful to cover up problems before they cause any unpleasantness.

The problem with this is that it is inherently dishonest. God created us for deep communion with another. We cannot achieve this when we hide parts of ourselves from others out of fear. Remember that "There is no fear in love. But perfect love drives out fear" (1 John 4:18). It may be difficult, but in God's timing each of us can work toward true honesty in all parts of our relationships—even when we think our revelation may be unsettling.

If we don't develop this type of honesty when a disagreement does surface, each person may be surprised and hurt by the other's "unreasonable" anger, and terrible, wounding things might be said by both persons.

Talking through disagreements is a lot easier than letting them get to the point where something that may be relatively minor tears you apart.

But as Christians you can trust each other not to intentionally hurt each other. And you can offer forgiveness to each other when you slip and say or do something to hurt or offend.

The secret is learning to make conflicts work for you instead of against you. You will become a little closer each time you settle a problem in a way both partners can live with.

There are several ways to deal with conflict. For example, one person may give in:

Marshall: Let's go to the movies tonight.

Latrice: I really had my heart set on staying home, but if it's important to you to go out tonight, I'll go.

Or it may be possible to work out a compromise that meets both people's needs:

Marshall: Let's go to the movies tonight.

Latrice: I really had my heart set on staying home, but if it's important to you to go out tonight, I'll go.

Marshall: Well, if you want to stay home, maybe I will come over and watch a movie on television with you.

Latrice: That sounds like a pretty good idea.

Sometimes you will not be able to agree on certain issues. That can be a real test of your love and trust for each other. It's a time to say, "I love you even if I don't agree with you." If you can practice this kind of acceptance with people around you, it will be a lot easier to do in a marriage relationship. You don't always have to agree about everything. (Of course, if the issue involves a matter of right and wrong, a clear command of God, you will want to keep on witnessing for the right, striving lovingly to change the other person's point of view and praying for God's Spirit to work through your witness.)

Can We Talk to Each Other with Complete Honesty?

One of the joys of a good relationship is having someone to talk to. The freer you feel to share about yourself with another person, the closer you will feel toward that person. All of us are at different levels, though, when it comes to what we think is complete honesty. You may want to share your innermost thoughts. The other person may have to think through an issue before sharing it with anybody.

What If We Belong to Different Churches?

The question may be, Can a marriage work if the partners are of a different religion? Yes, but it's not easy. The ideal is to be equally committed to Christ and both belong to the same church so that you can share your faith completely. Christ should be the cornerstone of a relationship—certainly of a marriage. It is unfortunate when one or the other cannot share Him because of differences in belief or denomination.

Remember that if you want a Christian marriage, marry a committed Christian. A marriage that is built on a deep trust in and communion with God is like no other relationship on this earth. When both partners seek God's will in their lives, they are not alone in their struggle to make their marriage work. Their shared faith is the basis for all goals, all values, all decisions. God provides them with the strength they need when trouble comes; He guides them to the abundant life He wants for all of us.

Chapter 7

When Two Become One

This is the part you are waiting for, right? Or maybe you aren't that eager for marriage. Is it really all it's cracked up to be? Think back to the creation story you read in the beginning of this book. When God created the first man and woman, He blessed them and invited them to join together in sexual union and to multiply. This original blessing isn't something to scoff at. Rather, it is far more powerful and wonderful than most people imagine!

What actually happens in sexual intercourse?

What difference does marriage make in a sexual relationship?

How often does a married couple have intercourse?

What is the secret of a happy marriage?

What Happens in Sexual Intercourse?

Sexual intercourse is more than placing the penis in the vagina. When God says that a man and woman become one flesh, it means they share all things in the most deep and intimate ways. Emotions, thoughts, desires, hopes, dreams—all are shared in the marriage bed. The Bible put it this way: "Has not the Lord made them one? In flesh and spirit they are His" (Malachi 2:15).

When a married couple comes together intimately, there is a time before intercourse when the couple stroke, touch, gently massage, and kiss each other's bodies. This is called **foreplay**. Ideally, they have talked about what arouses each of them and know which areas of the body to stimulate. These areas, called **erogenous zones**, are a little different for each person. Typically they include the sex organs and the areas around them, the nipples, inner thighs, mouth, lips, neck, earlobes, eyelids—all areas with many nerve endings. As the couple becomes more and more excited, heartbeat and blood pressure go up dramatically. Muscles tense. In some people, a measles-like flush covers part of their bodies. In about 60 percent of men and nearly 100 percent of women, nipples become erect and enlarged.

Blood rushes into the man's penis and stays there, making it erect and hard. The woman's vagina expands and produces a lubricating fluid that makes intercourse easier. The muscles at the entrance to the vagina relax. Her clitoris enlarges at first, flattens out, and then seems to disappear under the fold of skin that ordinarily covers most of it.

When both partners are ready, they work together to guide the penis into the vagina. As the penis moves back and forth inside the vagina there is friction on the clitoris caused by the movement of the labia.

Their excitement may build until one or both of them experience orgasm. The man's penis ejaculates semen; the woman's vagina contracts and expands several times; they tremble with intense physical and emotional pleasure.

Then all of the signs of arousal go away. A feeling of well-being and complete relaxation floods their bodies. This can be a special time of tenderness when they can lie in each other's arms, caressing and talking.

There may also be relief and peace that comes from the security of the marriage relationship. The couple can rest assured that the promises to love, honor, and cherish are in place, making it safe to be so vulnerable as during intercourse. In marriage, such times of intimacy affirm the bonds of love.

Is It Always Like That?

No. Different couples have different preferences about such things as foreplay and position during intercourse. There are many variations.

People have described intercourse as thrilling, soul-stirring, boring, shocking, deeply satisfying, painful, wonderfully comfortable, humiliating, confidence-building, disappointing, fascinating, disgusting, and delightful.

How can the same experience be so different for different people?

God intends intercourse to be a superbly joyous way to express mature committed love between a man and a woman. In many different places, the Bible speaks very positively of sexual intercourse—always within marriage. (Different words are used to describe sex outside of marriage.) Does this mean that sex within marriage always feels wonderful and sex without marriage always feels terrible?

It isn't quite that simple. Researchers are finding that sex without commitment tends to be flat and joyless compared to sex within a good marriage. Notice the word *good*. Marriage alone does not do it. More is necessary.

What Things Make a Difference in Sexual Pleasure?

The couple's total relationship controls their ability to give and receive sexual pleasure. Before intercourse can be the great experience it is meant to be, couples need to have complete trust and confidence in each other. They need to know that they are loved. Then each is free to suggest having intercourse, and each can say "some other time," without the other feeling rejected.

If an unmarried man and woman try to use intercourse to become closer to each other, they will be disappointed. In marital intercourse, a couple celebrates the unity—the concern for each other's needs—that already is there. Apart from marriage, this same activity can produce doubt and insecurity because two unmarried people have no such safety and security with each other. In a sense, rather than strengthen their bond, they weaken it because they have told lies with their bodies.

Even within a good relationship, the quality and intensity of a sexual experience varies greatly from one time to another. Sometimes the pair will come to orgasm together, sometimes separately. Sometimes one person will enjoy intercourse but will not come to orgasm at all.

For most people, the most important part of a sexual relationship is emotional intimacy. Their deepest needs are met by tenderness, closeness, and sharing. This is why the Book of Malachi talks about the union of flesh and spirit. This kind of emotional intimacy can only happen in a committed marriage.

Love . . . "Till Death Do Us Part"

"Love is patient,

love is kind.

It does not envy,

it does not boast,
it is not proud.

It is not rude,

it is not
self-seeking,

it is not easily angered,

it keeps no record of wrongs.

Love does not delight in evil
but rejoices with the truth.

It always protects, always trusts,
always hopes, always perseveres.

Love never fails."

I Corinthians 13:4–8a

Eager though we may be to have needs met and dreams fulfilled, we do not demand instant satisfaction to all our desires. We remind ourselves that a relationship that does not continue to grow is dying. Ours will grow—because our marriage is worth our energy and attention.

We will always listen to each other. We will call on God's power to work within us as we try to understand and meet the other's needs.

Daily, we'll tell and show each other: You are the most important person in my life. Secure in the other's love, we will not allow lesser relationships to threaten us.

Because we recognize that all talents and successes are gifts from God, neither of us needs to "win," to be the most important one in the world's eyes.

We will give each other the same politeness, consideration, and attention we give to a most honored guest.

For each of us, the other's needs will be as important as our own.

Recognizing that irritability is often caused by suppressed anger or worry, we will try to be open with each other about how we really feel. Because we care about each other, we will control words and actions that might hurt the other.

Sometimes we will fail; sometimes we will hurt each other. But as forgiven sinners, we can forgive those wrongs without getting even and without keeping score.

Because Christ lives in us, we can encourage each other to study His Word and live in His light.

We give total, lifelong commitment to this marriage and to each other. Even if bad times come, we will not give up; we will struggle and pray and love and grow.

We are one in Christ—forever.

In 1 Corinthians 13:4–8a, we see the qualities of biblical masculinity and femininity displayed. Focused on Christ, we begin to love others as He loves us. This love is quick to apologize for failures and does not keep a record of others' failures toward us. The humility evident in such a self-giving love frees others to love us in the same way.

As you mature into adulthood, consider keeping these verses handy. They describe the type of love we are to show all others, not just our spouse. This kind of love changes the world.

Why Does a Piece of Paper—A Marriage Certificate—Make a Difference?

The marriage certificate is a public commitment to make the relationship work, "for better or for worse." You say to each other: No matter what happens, I will be there. If a child is conceived, we accept responsibility for that child together.

The reason weddings have witnesses—often a church full of them—is that the health of each individual marriage also impacts the health of the community. If you reject your marriage vows, you hurt more than just your spouse. You are weakening the entire community, which often has to work very hard to mitigate the damage of a failed marriage. One study found that just one divorce costs the state as much as $30,000. The emotional and spiritual costs are even higher.

Some people are afraid of marriage since it means total commitment and total vulnerability. If you choose unwisely, you will be badly hurt. If both partners hold back a little, afraid to risk too much of themselves, complete intimacy will not happen—emotionally or sexually. Outside the security of a lifetime commitment, any problem triggers anxiety—and the anxiety itself can be a barrier to mutual sexual fulfillment.

God intends that a man and a woman will "become one flesh" (Genesis 2:24) in marriage. The feelings of oneness in sexual intercourse do not necessarily happen overnight. Sometimes years of loving communication and continual adjustment are needed to reach a completely satisfying sexual relationship.

How Often Does a Young Married Couple Have Intercourse?

There are such wide differences among individuals that it is impossible to come up with a definition of what is normal.

Even for the same person, sexual desire will vary. Much depends on how one feels on a given day. As years go by, urgent physical needs often give way to the desire for a more complete but less frequent, emotional and physical experience. On the other hand, a woman's **sex drive** may be stronger when she is in her 30s and 40s. Most men and women are physically capable of sexual activity until death.

While it is common for young newlyweds to focus on frequency of intercourse, especially if they have saved sexual relations for marriage, the more important question is whether each time of intimacy is marked by self-giving love. Some people mistakenly believe having lots of sex in marriage is the key to happiness, but troubles will surely arise if either spouse is simply using the other for his or her own sexual pleasure. If we are to view marital love in light of Christ's relationship to the Church, we know that any selfish advances will lead us to less than what God has in store for us.

Building a Good Marriage

So many marriages are unhappy. How can we make ours a good one?

Build your marriage on Christ; then it will not crumble when trouble comes. Jesus promised that "where two or three come together in My name, there am I with them" (Matthew 18:20). Of course, this is true in any group of Christians, but think of the power His promise adds to the intimate relationship of marriage! God works in and through each partner, helping each to find the true meaning of love, "that your joy may be complete" (John 15:11).

St. Paul compares Christian marriage to Christ's relationship with us, His Church (Ephesians 5:21–33). Christ's love is the model for the love we are to have toward our mate: love that gives itself away, love that does not depend on the other doing anything or being anything, love that is totally without strings, love that does not have to be earned in any way.

Of course Christians, like anyone else, are affected by the times in which they live. Old-fashioned marriages were far less likely to end in divorce than marriages today. Each person had clearly spelled-out duties, and neither expected more than a reasonable amount of comfort and security.

People today expect marriage to be a loving, deeply intimate joining of two equal partners. That's much more demanding than the old-style marriage. The partners must work together to set realistic goals for themselves:

When will we have children? How many? How will we care for them?

How will we handle our money? How will we decide what we can afford? What if we disagree?

How will we divide household tasks? Will we do it the way our parents did or develop our own patterns?

Where will we live? Will we both have careers outside our home? How will we share in leisure activities? What material things (house, cars, etc.) do we want? How will we make sure we make God a part of our home? What will we do to serve and praise Him?

Once you have chosen your goals, you will need to decide which ones are most important. Some goals probably must be sacrificed or postponed to make others possible. When you decide to have children, you will have to look also at what the commitment to being a parent means for each of you.

Once decisions are made, the solutions are not necessarily permanent. Children have different needs at different stages. People change. Situations change. But God's promises remain the same. Jesus has committed Himself to remain with us always. He will help you handle all that comes your way.

Submit to one another out of reverence for Christ.
Ephesians 5:21

Chapter 8

When Two Become Three

As you mature and grow into a woman after God's heart, you will find that marriage provides ample opportunities to become more Christlike. A person once called marriage "God's training ground for love." If this is true for marriage, how much more so when a person becomes a parent! The daily effort to care for and nurture children is full of rewards and challenges like few other experiences in life.

You may feel like you aren't ready to be a parent and may never be ready for such an awesome responsibility. You may wonder if you even want children. Wouldn't it be more fun to just be married without kids?

Think back to the creation account in Genesis. God's first blessing to the new man and woman was that they "be fruitful and increase in number; and fill the earth" (Genesis 1:28). This wasn't a curse or a burden, although their sin led to more struggle in all relationships involving people and pain in childbirth for the woman. Rather, God the Creator invited humans to participate in His ongoing creation by bringing forth new living beings. Remember Malachi 2:15: "Has not the LORD made them one? In flesh and spirit they are His. And why one? Because He was seeking godly offspring."

While being a parent may be the most rewarding experience of your life, it's not something most people can step into without preparation. This chapter aims to answer some common questions about what having and raising children is about.

When should we have a child?

What are some challenges of having children?

What happens in childbirth?

Why are so many new parents tired and depressed?

Should married couples use birth control to avoid having children?

Questions about Becoming Parents

When is the best time to start a family?

The honest answer is that there may never be one best time. And if there is, it still may take several months for a couple to conceive and another nine months before the child is born. In that span of time, circumstances may have changed, and the time may not be as ideal as it once was.

Perhaps a better way to think about this is to examine whether both parents have cultivated in themselves and their marriage the love, service, and self-sacrifice that provide the best foundation for bringing children into the world. However, even if a person is still a "work in progress" (and doesn't this describe all of us?), having children isn't something to fear or avoid.

Perhaps the "best time to have children" also describes what you should be working toward as a married couple: being secure in your relationship as husband and wife, having worked through the financial, emotional, and spiritual commitment necessary to be both good marriage partners and good parents.

Many couples, however, find themselves surprised by the joy of pregnancy without having worked all this out perfectly. This time of preparation can be an incredible time of bonding (and challenges) as the couple works all these issues out.

What are some of the challenges of having children?

For one child, you must be ready for a 24-hour-a-day, 18-year commitment. If you want several children, more years are involved. There is little to prepare a person for the kind of commitment being a parent requires, but most parents adapt after the initial shock and sleeplessness.

Children are delightful, loving, cuddly charmers. They also whine, have nightmares, fight with each other, and test your patience to the limit. Since children are immature, it is important that parents be mature. God both blesses us and teaches us through our children. As we respond to our children's needs, we find we can be wiser, more patient, and more unselfish than we would have thought possible.

Having a child to give as a gift to your husband or to strengthen a shaky marriage is the wrong reason and can cause many problems for you, your husband, and your child.

How can a woman tell whether she's pregnant?

Doctors look for an increase in the size of the uterus and the breasts. The cervix may be softer and may have a bluish tint. They also test the blood or the urine for a hormonal change that can be detected about 10 days after conception.

The woman may have noticed any or all of these symptoms: a missed period, breast fullness and tenderness, pre-breakfast nausea, unusual tiredness, frequency of urination. However, all these symptoms may have other causes. It is possible (but unusual) for a pregnant woman to have a normal period.

While home pregnancy tests are readily available today, their accuracy rate is not 100 percent. Since early diagnosis of pregnancy is very important, it is far better to see a physician. There are many substances—medicines, cigarette smoke, alcohol, drugs—that can severely damage the developing fetus. Pregnant mothers who are in top physical condition have much healthier babies and are less likely to have problems themselves.

What happens after the egg and the sperm meet in the fallopian tube?

The fertilized egg fastens itself to the cushiony wall of the uterus. A thin, tough bag called the **amnion** forms around the egg. It is filled with a watery liquid called amniotic fluid. The developing baby (called an **embryo** at this stage) floats in the liquid, which protects it from bumps or changes in temperature.

At the end of two months, the embryo has a brain, eyes, ears, heart, liver, arms, legs—not fully developed yet, but recognizable. After the eighth week, the embryo is called a fetus. By this time, a flat network of blood vessels, the **placenta**, has formed on the uterus wall. Mother and fetus have separate bloodstreams. The placenta is close to the mother's blood vessels so that food and oxygen can filter through it to the **umbilical cord** and on to the fetus. Waste materials take the same route back to the mother's bloodstream.

During the third and fourth months, nails begin to form on fingers and toes. Sex organs develop. The mother has the thrilling experience of feeling a little flutter inside her as the baby moves. As the fetus continues to grow, the mother's uterus and abdomen stretch to many times their original size. She becomes more and more conscious of the baby moving inside her.

How is the baby's sex decided?

All human cells, including sperm and egg cells, have 23 pairs of **chromosomes**. The chromosomes each contain many genes, different characteristics that are passed on to the next generation. About half of a man's sperm cells have a male chromosome; the other half have a female chromosome. The question of male or female depends on which sperm happens to reach the egg cell first.

What decides color of hair, musical ability, intelligence—all the things people inherit from their parents?

People inherit possibilities from their parents—possibilities that they may or may not develop in life. These possibilities may include athletic, intellectual, and musical abilities. Most of us inherit far more natural talent than we ever use. However, all these possibilities are in the new cell that forms when the sperm meets the egg. A woman's body makes hundreds of egg cells in her lifetime, each with a different combination of genes. Some genes carry characteristics she does not have herself, such as red hair like her great-grandfather's.

A man's body makes millions of sperm cells in his lifetime, each with a different combination of genes from his family. The baby's characteristics will depend on which sperm cell meets which egg cell. One of the special wonders of parenthood is seeing some of your own characteristics blended with those of the person you love best, creating a totally unique individual.

What happens in childbirth?

Powerful muscles in the uterus contract for 30 seconds or so, then relax. The contractions feel like a mild menstrual cramp and are about 15–20 minutes apart at first but gradually become stronger and closer together. The uterus is slowly pushing the baby downward. At some point, the bag of amniotic fluid breaks and the liquid flows out through the vagina.

Gradually the cervix opening expands from about 1/8 inch to about 4 inches. More contractions push the baby down into the vagina. The mother contracts her abdominal muscles to push; often the father helps by holding her and encouraging her. Many parents-to-be attend classes that prepare them for this moment.

The baby's head usually appears first, then one shoulder followed by the other. The doctor guides and supports—but never pulls—the baby.

When the baby is breathing normally, the umbilical cord is cut about 3 inches from the abdomen. In time, the stump will dry up and fall off, leaving a navel behind.

Its work finished, the placenta is now expelled from the mother's body. The entire birth process ordinarily takes about 8–20 hours for a first child.

Is childbirth painful?

Pregnant women who are well-informed about what to expect tend to be more relaxed and therefore experience less pain. Many women learn exercises and breathing techniques that give them some control over the process, and they like that. But each individual is different. Some women choose to take medication to help them control the pain during labor.

Is it harder to give birth to twins or triplets?

Not really. Because she is carrying more weight, the mother may be a little more uncomfortable during the last month or so. But the babies are born one at a time. Since they are likely to be smaller than other babies, they may need special care for a while.

What is the difference between identical twins and fraternal twins?

Fraternal twins are conceived when two different sperm cells join two different egg cells. Although they often feel especially close to each other, they each inherited a different set of characteristics from their parents.

Identical twins are conceived when one sperm cell joins one egg cell. The fertilized cell splits into two or more cells that are exactly alike, and each of these divided cells grows into a separate individual. Although identical twins begin life with the same set of inherited characteristics, they have different experiences and make different choices. Each becomes a unique individual, exactly like no one else in the world. Each has his or her own special relationship with God.

If children are a gift from God, why are so many new parents tired and depressed?

All new parents get tired, since the new member of the family is apt to sleep all day and howl all night. Caring for a new baby is a *lot* of work, especially during the first month or two. Normal hormonal changes in a new mother's body also can cause depression. Some mothers who quit jobs for parenting find it hard to get used to staying at home. Some find it helpful to take a college course, or do volunteer work—anything that adds some mental stimulation and adult companionship to their lives.

New parents can become upset because they don't measure up to their own ideals of what a good parent should be and do. They can't always soothe the baby when he or she is crying. Perhaps the mother is unable to nurse the baby as she had hoped. When they stop trying to be superparents, they'll enjoy parenting more.

Sometimes new parents need professional guidance as they struggle to adjust. They may seek out prayer and counsel from a pastor, their own parents, or older friends who have already experienced similar struggles. If parents continue to have difficulties adjusting to the demands of being a parent, they may benefit from the services of a trained Christian counselor who can help them get to the core issues bothering them.

Even normal parents sometimes have mixed feelings about their baby. They love their baby, yet sometimes they don't *like* him or her very much. They may resent the changes the baby has brought to their lives or feel trapped, weighed down by responsibility. If they give each other love, understanding, and support, this shared experience will end up being a very positive one. Talking about feelings helps. So does prayer. As time goes on, the new parents will find that, although feelings of irritation and anger come and go, their love for their child is a basic, growing part of their love for each other and for God.

What is a miscarriage?

Sometimes a fetus does not develop properly, so the uterus pushes it out of the body. This is called a miscarriage and is most likely to happen during the second or third month of pregnancy. Natural miscarriages happen to many women, and many of them may not even know they are pregnant when it happens. For those who are already aware of the child growing inside them, a miscarriage can bring deep heartache and sadness.

What is a premature baby?

Some babies are born before the nine months are up. If a baby is born more than a month early, she or he will probably weigh less than 5½ pounds. Babies that small may need special care to survive. A baby weighing less than 2 pounds has only a small chance of survival, although new medical techniques now make it possible for doctors to save smaller and smaller babies.

What causes birth defects?

Some defects are inherited; others are caused by outside factors such as drugs, infection, STDs, alcohol, smoking, poor nutrition, radiation, or pollutants. The risks are greater for pregnant women under 18 or over 35. Early diagnosis of pregnancy is important because commonly prescribed medicines may be harmful to a developing fetus. The father's exposure to some chemicals can cause birth defects in babies conceived while the chemical remains in the father's body.

Women who have what is called Rh-negative blood cells also risk birth defects in their second pregnancy. If the fetus has Rh-positive blood, the mother's body will attack the fetus's red blood cells. This can be prevented by vaccination after the birth of a first baby or after a miscarriage.

Everyone should have a complete physical examination before marriage. For women, the exam should include blood tests to check immunity to rubella and to find out blood type. Babies born to mothers who have rubella (German measles) during pregnancy often have serious birth defects. Doctors recommend that females be vaccinated against rubella while they are young girls, long before they conceive a child. A woman should not become pregnant until at least three months after vaccination.

Why are some couples unable to have a child?

In many cases the causes of infertility are unknown. Some people delay childbearing until their 30s or 40s, and their chances of conceiving a child decrease the older they are. There are a number of diseases and infections that can damage the reproductive organs. However, couples who fail to conceive within the first two years of unprotected intercourse have a better chance than ever before of achieving conception with medical help. If they seek treatment, many will succeed in conceiving.

Should married couples use birth control to avoid conceiving children?

Considering the command and blessing of God to the first couple to bring forth children, couples today should enter marriage with the intent to welcome any children God may give them. However, there may be times during the marriage when it may be wise to avoid a pregnancy, such as times of extreme financial hardship, emotional or mental instability, or in the midst of long-term marital discord.

There are a variety of contraceptives available for couples to use today, ranging from condoms, to birth control pills or patches, to barrier products such as a diaphragm, to natural family planning. These methods have varying levels of effectiveness, but none is 100-percent effective.

But aren't there too many people in the world already? I hear about overpopulation on the news and worry that humans are causing a lot of problems for the planet.

The truth is that many nations are facing a crisis precisely because they are not having enough children. European women are having so few children that no nation on the entire continent can sustain even a basic replacement rate of 2.1 children per woman. Even the United States has fallen below replacement level for the first time. What this means is that there won't be enough workers to fill all the jobs, and there will be more people receiving Social Security than those who can pay into the system.

It is a serious danger to build society around principles that contradict God's plan for humans, in this case around the idea that children are not to be valued and lovingly welcomed into every home.

Shouldn't I learn more about birth control now in case I find myself in a situation where I need it?

Our culture works hard to convince young people to learn about birth control so they can have "safe sex." God has a different idea. He teaches us that we are all part of His divine plan for loving intimate communion within the boundaries of marriage. He also teaches us that we can train ourselves to respect and care for others with the same self-giving love He extends to us. We all have a choice to make daily— whether we will receive and embrace the gifts God gives us or reject them and try to carve out a life apart from Him.

Chapter 9

Tough Questions

You may be thinking that if you could live a life like the one described in these pages, it would be pretty nice. Or you may wonder if it is possible to really live out God's calling for sexuality and relationships. It may seem like a fairy tale when you look around at the pain and sorrow of the real world. How does all this measure up against the really tough questions?

What if I get pregnant?

What actually happens in an abortion?

How can a sexy magazine or an R-rated movie possibly hurt me?

Why do promiscuous people act the way they do?

What causes homosexuality?

How do I know if I am in an abusive relationship?

Most of this chapter zeros in on questions you have probably thought about at one time or another. The questions cover a wide range of topics.

Can sperm swim through jeans?

Social workers who operate a telephone question-answering service report that this is the most common question asked by teen callers. It is very unusual for a woman to get pregnant without sexual intercourse. However, it is a possible result of heavy stimulation. If sperm are deposited on the vulva, they may travel into the vagina and on through to the uterus to a fallopian tube.

Many unplanned pregnancies have begun when people had sexual intercourse in what they've been told is a "safe" way or when they use birth control methods incorrectly.

Pregnancy *can* happen

—the first time a person has intercourse.
—after intercourse in any position.
—on *any* day of a woman's menstrual cycle.
—even though the woman does not come to orgasm.

A woman *cannot* prevent pregnancy by

—taking a birth control pill that morning.
—standing for an extended period immediately after intercourse.
—putting a tampon in the vagina first.
—**douching** (washing out the vagina) with cola or anything else. (This can cause an infection.)

A man *cannot* prevent pregnancy by

—using plastic wrap or a plastic bag to catch the semen.
—withdrawing his penis just before ejaculating. (This is very unreliable because sperm can leave the penis before ejaculation.)

Looking at all these scenarios, it's clear that many will try just about anything to circumvent God's design for sexuality. It begs the question why a godly person would be in such a situation anyway. It may seem impossible to live a life of purity, but with God's help, it isn't. It takes practice, patience, prayer, and persistence. When you find yourself getting close to a sexually charged situation, it may help to ask, Does this situation lead me closer to or farther from my relationship with God?

I'm not married, and I think I got pregnant. What should I do? Where can I go for help? I CAN'T tell my parents.

Right now you are probably feeling panicky, guilty, and worried sick. Maybe you think you have destroyed your relationship with your parents—or even your relationship with God. Are you wondering whether your parents will ever forgive you? Will God forgive you?

God will. Talk to Him about what you have done and how you feel. Jesus didn't even scold the woman caught in the act of adultery. Instead, He protected her from those who would harm her and sent her home with the words, "leave your life of sin" (John 8:11).

Jesus will forgive both you and the baby's father—and gladly welcome you back. Remember the parable of the lost sheep (Luke 15:1–7). Jesus will stick by you in the difficult times ahead.

Remember, too, that God works through other people—your parents, for instance.

If you feel unable to talk to your parents right now, you might try talking to

- **a pastor or church youth worker,**
- **a school counselor or school nurse,**
- **your family doctor or a doctor at a clinic.**

Professional ethics—and, often, state laws—forbid any of the professionals listed above from telling your parents without your consent. However, whoever you talk to probably will urge you to confide in your parents without delay. Following are some good reasons to talk to your parents.

Your parents are likely to be more supportive, more helpful, more forgiving than you think. Yes, they may be angry and hurt at first. But they will be even more hurt when they find out later that you have shut them out of this crisis in your life.

They are almost certain to find out sooner or later. Even now, they are probably uneasily aware that something is wrong. When you lie to someone you love, you move further and further away from them. The secret makes a wall between you and people who love you very deeply.

You will be facing some important decisions that will profoundly affect the lives of several people, including your unborn child. Help and support will be very important as you explore the consequences of each option open to you and as you think through the moral issues involved so that someday you can look back and say, "I made the right choice."

A caring, professionally trained Christian counselor can help you, your parents, and your baby's father understand one another better. Even when parents try hard to forgive and understand, they can't easily get rid of their feelings of anger, disappointment, and failure. This will be a very painful time for all of you, and you need all the support you can get.

Mollie knows for sure she is pregnant. She says she wants to keep her baby. Is that a good idea?

That depends. Single parent families can work if the parent is well prepared for the responsibility of a child. Enough money, enough maturity, enough emotional and physical strength—all these are essential.

Some unwed mothers look forward very much to having a baby to love. "The baby will always love me," they figure. "I'd much rather take care of a baby than go to school!"

But the baby is much more work than school ever was. The longed-for love grows slowly and depends on the care and attention she is able to give the baby. Money may be hard to come by. Jobs are scarce without a good education, but going back to school is tough when babysitting arrangements must be made.

Mollie may one day find herself trapped with a monotonous lifestyle. And her child would suffer most of all. Newspaper columnists often print pathetic letters from young people who must deal with the problem of a much-too-early pregnancy.

However, she may also find incredible support from her family and friends. It doesn't make a difficult situation stress-free, but it does help. God can work good out of the toughest situations, but certainly no one should intentionally engage in actions that would bring about such difficulties.

Mollie and her boyfriend might decide to get married. Then the baby will have two parents.

Not necessarily. Many marriages that start this way end in divorce. Any time two people enter marriage without their full commitment to love through thick and thin, their chances of failure increase. A marriage founded solely on an unintended pregnancy may be tricky to maintain.

Even if the marriage lasts, the chances of a happy relationship are slim—and both are likely to unconsciously blame the baby. Parents who feel their lives have been stunted by the responsibility of a child find it very difficult to meet that child's needs.

Should Mollie give her baby up for adoption?

Only Mollie can decide that. She must compare the love and care she is able to give her child with what adoptive parents can give. Mollie's own feelings, and those of the child's father, also must be considered.

These days, many unwed mothers decide to keep their babies. If there are several unwed mothers in a school, they are likely to encourage one another to make the same choices. If Mollie decides to give up her baby, she may be making an unpopular decision but one that will bring joy to a couple who may have been waiting for years for a baby. Church-affiliated adoption agencies have long been placing babies in Christian homes. However, it is certainly true that none of the options available to Mollie are without pain.

What about abortion? I hear there's nothing to it these days.

What you've heard is only partly true. Medically speaking, **abortion** is a simple procedure if done within the first three months of pregnancy. However, abortion clinics are not regulated as strictly as hospitals, and there are greater risks when having an abortion done there. Sadly, in many states, free or low-cost clinics make it possible for teens to get abortions without the consent or knowledge of their parents.

In other words, Mollie is free to make an irreversible decision without the support of people who love her very much. Although abortion may seem the easiest way out of Mollie's dilemma, it is not. Killing an embryo or fetus is not like having an infected tooth pulled. Mollie is dealing with a living being, created by God just as she herself was created by God. Even those who don't care about the judgment of God's Word may experience guilt, grief, and psychological and emotional scars that take a long time to heal. Most people considering abortion never have heard stories of the pain and guilt others have experienced who have gone through with an abortion.

What actually happens in an abortion?

In early pregnancy, the most common method is vacuum aspiration. A plastic tube is inserted into the uterus. The developing baby and menstrual fluids are vacuumed out. In the dilation and curettage method (often called D&C), a sharp spoon-shaped instrument scrapes away pieces of the pre-born child until it is all gone. RU-486 is a drug that expels the embryo from the uterus. Saline abortion is often used after the first three months of pregnancy. A needle inserted into the uterus draws out some amniotic fluid. This fluid is replaced with a saline (salt) solution that kills the fetus. Within 24 hours, the dead fetus is expelled from the mother's body.

What does the Bible say about abortion?

The Bible says that each of us has a special relationship with God that began *before we were born.* Jeremiah writes:

"The word of the LORD came to me, saying, 'Before I formed you in the womb I knew you, before you were born I set you apart; I appointed you as a prophet to the nations'" (Jeremiah 1:4–5).

David, the psalm writer and king, is even more specific:

"You created every part of me; you put me together in my mother's womb. . . . When my bones were being formed, . . . when I was growing there in secret, you knew that I was there—you saw me before I was born. The days allotted to me had all been recorded in your book, before any of them ever began" (Psalm 139:13–16 TEV).

The Bible also emphasizes the value of each human life. "You shall not murder" (Exodus 20:13) is one of the Ten Commandments God wrote with His own hand and gave in a special way to His people.

There is no way to justify killing a human embryo or fetus—even though some claim an abortion is justified if it saves the mother (and father) from embarrassment, broken plans for the future, or emotional pain. But God values all life. Life is so special that God sent His own Son to be born of a young human mother so all people could share His love on earth and have eternal life in heaven.

What is pornography?

Some of the most beautiful statues or pictures portray the naked human body. They give us an appreciation for how wonderfully God has made us. Unfortunately, humans take this beauty and distort it; all too often we make ourselves less than we are intended to be.

If, when you look at a picture (or statue or the like), you can easily remember that it shows a special person who is valued by God, this is not pornography. **Pornography** happens when a human is displayed as a sex object, a thing to be used for someone else's pleasure. It is degrading and disrespectful. Pornography makes us feel dirty, uneasily guilty about our sexuality, instead of proud and grateful that God has made us male or female.

Is it really wrong to just look? How can a picture, magazine, or movie hurt me?

Consider where your Christian attitudes, opinions, and values come from. You weren't born with them. Indeed, God's Word reminds us that we all have an inborn leaning toward sin. (See, for example, Ephesians 2:3 and 4:22.) On the basis of the Bible, we call this "our old sinful flesh." We know, too, from God's Word that the devil seeks to work through the world—the evil influences all about us—to lead God's people to sin and lack of trust in God.

By Baptism, God made us His own children—forgiven people who are called to resist the devil and the sinful world.

The question then becomes: Is pornography part of the world, which appeals to our sinful flesh? Or is it part of God's good creation, which appeals to our new nature and builds our spiritual life?

While pornography may seem exciting and thrilling, especially at first, it can pollute our minds in the same way sewage pollutes a river— our minds and souls are slowly being poisoned. Many young people are finding themselves addicted to Internet pornography without realizing how they got there. Because their mind was still forming when they poisoned it, they have difficulty finding healing. If you are in such a situation, seek out your pastor, your Christian friends, and a trained Christian counselor immediately.

What's wrong with R-rated movies? What if the movie is just frank and open, not dirty?

The best way to tell whether a movie is harmful is to notice the effect on your thinking. Does the movie picture a world in which God exists? Does it substitute a slick "get all you can" philosophy for honest love? Does it tear down or build Christian values?

Sometimes explicit language has a slightly different meaning from the more polite words. Constant use of street words for sex can make intercourse seem a hostile act instead of a way to express committed love.

We can decide whether to eat roast beef or garbage. We also have the power by God's Spirit to choose what goes into our heads and hearts. Read the "whatevers" in Philippians 4:8 as a guide to what we should think about.

Right. It's MY head, MY body. If I happen to get a kick out of a mildly dirty magazine, that's MY business.

Pay attention to the attitude behind these words above. Does this describe a person in a right relationship with Christ? Does this kind of thinking look like it leads to happiness?

God has not given you absolute ownership of your body.

"Do you not know that your body is a temple of the Holy Spirit, who is in you, whom you have received from God? You are not your own; you were bought at a price. Therefore honor God with your body" (1 Corinthians 6:19–20).

What is a flasher? Is he dangerous?

Flasher is a slang word for an **exhibitionist**, a person who gets sexual satisfaction from showing his or her genitals to others. The typical flasher is a man who delights in shocking young girls. Exhibitionists should be reported to the police so they can receive psychiatric help.

What if a woman is raped?

Rape happens when one person forces another to have sexual intercourse. Women and girls are usually the victims, although boys can be raped by both homosexual men or predatory women. Most psychologists feel that rape is a crime of violence, that a rapist wants to hurt and frighten a victim rather than get sexual pleasure.

A person who has been raped should go *immediately* to a hospital or a rape crisis center. A doctor will check him or her for injuries and will also look for evidence that the rape happened. In women, they look for sperm cells in the vagina. (No police report will be made without her consent. But if she delays or washes herself first, it may not be possible to prove anything.) The doctor also takes steps to prevent sexually transmitted disease.

The doctor also can recommend agencies that will provide free or inexpensive counseling. Victims need spiritual and emotional support as well as medical attention. A woman should seek help from her pastor or somebody she trusts as a committed Christian to receive the support in Christ that she needs.

How can a woman protect herself?

Many women believe that nothing can ever happen to them. They take chances that are foolish. But the best way for women to protect themselves is to stay away from dangerous situations, such as hitchhiking or walking alone at night. It's important to be alert so you will recognize danger when you see it.

As a godly woman, you can be on the lookout for suspicious situations if you are at a party or out with friends. You can also try to care for and protect other young women who may have had too much to drink or have otherwise put themselves in vulnerable situations.

What is incest?

Incest is having sexual relations with a member of your family or another close relative. It is a crime. Because of the prohibitions against incest, it is against the law to marry someone in one's immediate family—a brother or sister or father or mother. In many places, first cousins are not allowed to marry.

Incest is more common than most people think. It happens in all kinds of families—rich and poor, white and black, churchgoing and nonreligious.

Usually, an older person will convince a younger or weaker person that this twisted form of sex is okay or that any guilt belongs to the younger person. This is a betrayal of trust and is never true. The victim is not guilty and will probably suffer severe spiritual and psychological damage if the relationship continues.

She or he should firmly resist any future advances and should talk over the problem with a parent or pastor or other trusted counselor. The victim of incest needs help. And so does the aggressor.

What is a prostitute?

A **prostitute** is a person who engages in sexual activity for money or other goods, such as drugs or shelter. Most prostitutes are women; most customers are men.

There is a common but dangerous myth that most prostitutes have freely chosen to sell their bodies. Research shows that most have been physically or psychologically coerced into the trade. There is terrible abuse and trauma associated with it. Understanding prostitution requires us to look critically at our own culture as one that finds it acceptable to treat women as sexual objects. We also do well to recognize the responsibility of the men who create the demand that forces women into this sinful lifestyle.

Why do promiscuous people act the way they do?

A **promiscuous** person has sexual intercourse with many different partners. Although a promiscuous woman is usually looked down on in our culture, a promiscuous man may even be envied by some. However, researchers find very little difference in the personality and family backgrounds of these men and women. Their sex drive is no stronger than anyone else's, but they have a great need for something that will blot out their emotional problems.

Promiscuous people usually have very little self-confidence, accept little responsibility for their own behavior, and blame others for their own shortcomings. Because they do not take the time and effort to build a lasting relationship, they never discover how wonderful sex can be. Most sad of all, they are substituting sinful thrills for something much more thrilling: a close relationship with Jesus Christ that lasts eternally.

What are sadism and masochism?

In both, sex is linked with violence, twisting God's good gift into something vile and nasty. Either physical or psychological pain is made part of the sex act. A sadist likes to give pain; a masochist either wants pain or is willing to suffer anything to please the partner.

People who believe that sex is shameful and dirty are most vulnerable to this mental disorder. Some psychologists blame an increase in the numbers of sadists and masochists on the common approval of aggressiveness and even violence in our society. For instance, movies and TV shows often glorify violence and combine it with sex.

What is fetishism?

Nearly everyone finds certain things more sexually exciting than others. We may be aroused by a particular part of the body (hair, breasts), by an article of clothing, or (if you can believe the ads) by a certain perfume. For a fetishist (usually male), this preference turns into a compulsion. One particular object, often a piece of clothing, becomes "the loved one" for him and takes the place of a sex partner in his life. He will steal or even hurt someone in order to get it.

Another form of fetishism is *kleptomania*, compulsive stealing. Here the sick person is usually a woman who feels unloved and unwanted. She steals objects that have no value to her, other than the sexual excitement she gets from the act of stealing and from the object itself.

What is the difference between a transvestite and a transsexual? Are they homosexuals?

No. A **transvestite** is a person (usually male) who enjoys dressing in clothes of the opposite sex. Some habitually wear one item, like a bra or panties, under their own clothing. Others dress completely in women's clothing, either once in a while or—in extreme cases—all the time.

This behavior is a distortion and confusion of the order, purpose, and complementarity of the sexes that God clearly differentiates at creation. To blur the distinctions between men and women confuses the goodness of masculinity and femininity.

Transsexuals see themselves as the opposite sex; they feel trapped in the wrong body. They see the sex organs they were born with as deformities.

This disorder needs healing, confession, forgiveness, change of heart, right thinking, and a lot of grace. The treatment of transsexuality through a sex change operation is enabling serious sexual brokenness. You can't make a man into a woman with hormones and surgery—this just ignores what every XY chromosome in the body proclaims about who he is.

There is also some disagreement in the psychiatric community about whether transsexuality is about believing you are the opposite sex or if it is about the sexual excitement associated with being the other sex.

What about homosexuality?

Homosexuality is a broad term that covers a lot of areas, everything from having sexual attractions toward the same sex to engaging in sexual behavior with the same sex to taking on a gay or lesbian identity. Many people with same-sex attractions or behavior decide not to call themselves gay or lesbian. Some people have same-sex attractions or behavior for periods of time, and then the attractions diminish or end.

Is there a gay gene?

For years people talked about 10 percent of the population being gay; we now know that the number is somewhere between 1 to 3 percent. While there has been a lot of publicity about a "gay gene," no studies have ever found a genetic cause for homosexuality. Issues like sexual identity, attractions, and orientation are much too complicated to be attributed solely to a genetic cause, and the most recent research shows that homosexuality seems to be largely environmental.

Humans are not like machines that can be programmed to act in certain ways. There is always an element of choice or free will in human behavior—including human sexual behavior. So it would be incorrect to say that there is a "cause" for homosexuality. Homosexuality develops from a complex interaction between a person's temperament, environment, relationships, experiences, perceptions, and choices—and from the fact that we live in a fallen world. So each person's sexual development is different.

Having said that, there do seem to be some common factors for many people with same-sex attractions. Some people with same-sex attractions grew up not acting like or feeling connected to their same-sex peers. Some report early, inappropriate exposure to sex or pornography as children. And others report feeling disconnected from their same-sex parent or siblings.

Can a person change from homosexuality to heterosexuality?

What we do know, from many testimonies and studies, is that some people change their sexual orientation. Homosexuality is a changeable condition, and people who struggle with it should be allowed to change to live the way God intended them to. God uses a lot of different means to help people change. Prayer, obedience, healthy relationships, therapy, teaching, worship, confession, forgiveness, and His Spirit are all part of bringing healing and change in people's lives.

What does the Bible say about homosexuality?

The Bible clearly states that intimate sexual expression is intended between one man and one woman within the marriage relationship. Men and women are complementary, and when they come together in marriage, they become one flesh and there is the possibility of procreation. Two men together or two women together do not have this complementarity, and there is no possibility for procreation. Romans 1 teaches that **homosexual** behavior is one of the results of human sinfulness. Nowhere in the Bible is there any approval for homosexuality.

While we as Christians cannot condone homosexual behavior or identity, we will want to show compassion and love toward those who struggle with same-sex attractions. We will proclaim that God forgives all sin for Christ's sake and makes possible a new life through the power of the Holy Spirit. In fact, Scripture talks about those who used to act homosexually but have been washed, sanctified, and justified by God's Spirit (see 1 Corinthians 6:9–11).

As Christians, we also will avoid hurtful or mean behavior toward those who might be struggling with this issue. Sometimes other students are labeled "gay" or "lesbian" because of their appearance or because their interests are different from the norm. Such labels can follow a person for years and influence how he or she is treated by others. As Christians, we surely will avoid name-calling, gossip, bullying, or harassment.

How can I be sure I am not a homosexual?

Many young people worry unnecessarily about homosexual tendencies they suspect in themselves or about homosexual behavior in their past. They may have had one or more experiences with somebody of the same sex in which touching or other play resulted in orgasm. These experiences do not mean that someone is a homosexual.

It is also normal to have a deep attachment of friendship to someone of the same sex. David and Jonathan (see 1 Samuel 18), for instance, had a sincere love for each other that was very different from their normal sexual interest in the women they loved.

Many young people admire teachers or others who are the same sex. It is normal to admire someone very much and want to be near that person. Often this admiration helps you discover the direction you would like your own life to take.

Young people should not label themselves as homosexual. If you are worried about this, first share your concerns with your Father in heaven. Ask God to help you develop a healthy sense of identity rooted and grounded in Him, not in attractions or feelings that you have. Then talk to your pastor or another adult about your feelings.

It often takes a long time for a young person to feel at ease with members of the other sex. Be patient with yourself. Remember that you are not the only one who fears rejection; others feel just as insecure as you do. Ask God to help you become more comfortable with your own sexuality and with your own sense of femininity. He will.

What about "safe sex," using a condom?

Medical studies show that condoms are not completely effective in preventing the sexual transmission of the HIV (AIDS) virus. Studies also confirm that condoms do not offer total protection from chlamydia and human papilloma virus, two serious STDs that many sexually active teenagers have. The only real "safe sex" is with a lifelong marriage partner, with both partners remaining faithful to their marriage vows.

What about sexual harassment?

The law says that no one, man or woman, has to put up with unwelcome sexual advances, requests for sexual favors, and other verbal or physical conduct of a sexual nature.

The sexual harassment law is aimed mostly at the workplace, but the courts have said that it also applies to schools when the behavior causes a student fear, anxiety, shame, or embarrassment or keeps the student from being able to attend school.

Does that mean it's against the law for a man to flirt or kid with a woman?

Of course not. But he does have to be aware of the effect it's having on her. Is his flirting or kidding unwelcome? Did he continue kidding even after you let him know you don't like it? Is he making school or work an uncomfortable place for you? If that kind of kidding around happens at a party rather than at school or work, it's probably not illegal—but it's still wrong.

My supervisor at work keeps asking me to go out with him. I'm running out of excuses.

Tell him directly, "I like working with you, but I don't want to date you." Don't make excuses; don't say anything that he might interpret as encouraging. If he persists, remind him that you've already said you are not interested and that sexual harassment is against the law. (Although most sexual harassment cases involve men who harass women, the law also applies to women who harass men.) If you are worried about losing your job, keep a diary describing exactly what happens between you.

What good will a diary do?

If you decide to tell the general manager what has been going on, your diary will be evidence that you are telling the truth. If you get angry at your supervisor for other reasons, you may be tempted to bring a sexual harassment charge against him out of revenge or emotional retaliation. Your diary will help you to keep to the exact truth of what happened—no more, no less.

What about the woman who leads a man on and then rejects him?

Both men and women need to be aware of the signals they are sending. What one sees as friendly teasing between buddies can be taken by the other as a come-on for a closer relationship. However, no mistaken signal can excuse the person who forces his attentions on another.

But what if a person gets so "hot" he can't stop himself?

That myth is popular among people who do not want to accept responsibility for their own actions. Controlling one's sexual drive is possible at any point from first arousal to orgasm.

What's the difference between just kidding around and sexual harassment? Everybody gets kidded sometimes.

If it feels like harassment to the victim, it has gone beyond kidding. Sexual harassment often leaves people feeling very depressed, afraid, and unable to trust others. Many students report that they no longer want to come to school after it has happened.

A nationwide survey of 1,632 high school students found that 85 percent of girls and 76 percent of boys reported being sexually harassed at school. Sexual comments, jokes, gestures, or looks were the most common form of harassment. Surveys show that 65 percent of girls and 42 percent of boys also have experienced unwelcome sexual touching, pinching, or grabbing.

What's meant by "date rape"?

Most rapes are committed by a trusted friend or date rather than by a stranger. The rapist may be a member of your church or the most popular person in the senior class.

Women need to understand the following:

- Rape can happen to anyone.

- A popular, well-liked guy can be a rapist, especially if he's not used to taking no for an answer.

- A man whose words or actions show that he doesn't respect women is not someone you should trust.

- Submissive and docile women are natural victims. If you allow someone to impose his choices and decisions on you, you are sending a message you may regret. It doesn't mean you are at fault for his sinful actions, however.

A woman's best protection against rape is to decide in advance what her sexual limits are and communicate them clearly and emphatically to her date. A rapist often begins with sexual harassment: unwanted touch, sexual jokes, comments with double meanings. He needs to hear a loud and clear message that the woman will leave immediately if this behavior continues.

Those who use alcohol or drugs are much less likely to keep control of the situation. Watch out for anyone who urges you to drink or experiment with drugs!

A rapist will often try to put the blame on the victim for "leading him on." But each person is responsible for his own actions. If a man attempts to force himself on a woman after the woman says no, it's rape! This is criminal behavior, not just a guy who got carried away.

Men need to understand the following:

- It is never okay to use force, coercion, alcohol, or drugs to pressure a woman into unwanted sexual contact. Such an act is a criminal offense.

- The amount of money you have spent on a woman entitles you to nothing.

- When a woman says no, no is what she means.

- If you enjoy violent movies, especially when the violence is directed at women, you may eventually and mistakenly begin to think of violence as a way of dealing with problems and frustrations.

- No matter how aroused you get, you are able to control your sexual behavior.

- If alcohol or drugs have taken away your ability to think clearly and use good judgment, you are still responsible for your behavior.

Rape is a terrible sin. Although God forgives all sins, including those of a sexual assailant, the victim's emotional and mental scars do not go away. Moreover, the victim may be forced to cope with an unwanted pregnancy, and the sad reality is that many in that situation choose abortion.

What are "date rape drugs"?

Those looking to take sexual advantage of others sometimes use drugs that cause impaired judgment or memory loss to assist in a sexual assault. Date rape drugs such as GHB can be difficult to detect when placed in a drink, and their effects are increased when received together with alcohol. These drugs also have been used to help people commit robbery, assault, and other crimes against both men and women. People can protect themselves against date rape drugs in the following ways:

Don't accept open drinks from other people; open containers yourself.

Keep your drink with you at all times.

Avoid sharing drinks or drinking from common containers that might contain drugs.

Don't drink anything that tastes or smells unusual. (GHB tastes salty.)

Stay with friends so you can watch out for one another.

What is an "abusive relationship"?

Why does she stay with him? He treats her like dirt.

What does he see in her? He's been a different person ever since they started going together.

People often cling to a sick relationship because they see it as better than being alone. When self-esteem gets low enough, it's easy to say, "This is all I deserve. If we break up, I'll never find anyone else who will love me." They forget that they are special people who are loved and valued by God. God can and will provide the courage to break free, the patience to endure a period of being alone, and the confidence needed to form a healthy relationship with someone new.

An abusive relationship is one in which there is a pattern of repeated verbal, emotional, or physical abuse by which one dating partner tries to control the other. A woman might threaten to break up with her male friend if he doesn't give up his other friends and outside interests and spend all his free time with her. A man might insist in making all the decisions or threaten violence if his female friend won't have sex with him.

Once a person gives in to any of these kinds of emotional blackmail, it becomes harder to stand up for her rights the next time. The abuser continues to do whatever it takes to make the dating partner toe the line.

If a woman allows a man to threaten violence or actually hurt her, that violence is likely to continue. There will be times when the abuser reforms and asks forgiveness, but he will almost always repeat the pattern of violence again and again. Only with outside help is the abuser likely to accept responsibility for his own behavior and learn new ways of dealing with stress and conflict.

How can I tell when I'm in an abusive relationship?
Does your dating partner . . .

- get angry easily and often?

- handle anger by destroying things or treating people roughly?

- constantly put you down?

- frequently embarrass you in front of your friends?

- refuse to believe he has really hurt you?

- brag about previous girlfriends?

- insist on making all the decisions that affect both of you?

- try to stop you from ordinary socializing with friends, visiting your family, or talking with members of the other sex?

- use threats to make you do what he wants? (I'll leave you; I'll tell everyone your secret; I'll hit you again; I'll kill myself.)

- make you feel you deserve to be punished or abused?

- isolate you from people who really care about you?

- get so upset when you express a different opinion that you always give in, just to keep peace?

If you said yes to even one of the above questions, you are in an abusive relationship and need to get help. If you do nothing, things will almost surely get worse. Don't even think about marrying a person who treats you badly. You deserve to have a relationship of equality and love, not one of dependence and fear.

Chapter 10

Prayer Starters

This chapter is a collection of Scripture, prayers, and thought-starters. We hope you'll use them as ways to begin talking with God about your sexuality and as reminders that you are not—and never will be—alone.

Not Good Enough

Fear not, for I have redeemed you; I have summoned you by name; you are Mine (Isaiah 43:1).

The truth is, I'm a failure. I often don't feel good enough. I know that sometimes I am not that much fun to be around. At times I don't like myself very much.

I know it's my own fault sometimes. I get so discouraged; I give up before I even start. Some days I hardly speak to anyone. Other times, something inside me makes me act stupid and silly—to get their attention, I guess.

Keep telling me I am Yours, Lord Jesus. Remind me—again and again—that You love me. Show me how I can change to become more like You. Give me opportunities to make friends—friends who also love and trust in You. Help me appreciate the specialness You have created within me. Help me to listen when You call my name.

Too Far, Too Soon

For what I do is not the good I want to do; no, the evil I do not want
to do—this I keep on doing. . . . The mind of sinful man is death, but
the mind controlled by the Spirit is life and peace (Romans 7:19; 8:6).

What happens to my good intentions when I'm with him? Why does
my desire for him override everything else? Because I am so much in
love with him, I forget plans for the future—my parents' love for me, my
own deep knowledge of right and wrong.

I wonder how he feels about our growing closer together. What does
he really want? I know we shouldn't go on like this, but what will he
think if I back off now? Maybe we should talk over what our limits ought
to be—but I wouldn't know how to begin.

God, thank You for my sexuality, for the body You have given me.
But I need more! For one thing, I need Your forgiveness for so often
misusing Your gifts. I need Your support and Your wisdom as I turn
around and begin again. Give me the right words to say to him about
how we feel about each other. Help me to be a godly woman.

Lord Jesus, I really do want Your Spirit to control my life. Help me
remember that tonight!

In Love, I Think

Shout for joy to the Lord, all the earth, burst into jubilant song with
music; make music to the Lord with the harp, with the harp and the
sound of singing, with trumpets and the blast of the ram's horn—
shout for joy before the Lord, the King (Psalm 98:4–6).

Lord, what is this wonderful feeling? When I'm near him, my
bones melt. My heart pounds. I feel dizzy. Is this truly love or just
the excitement of getting to know someone who really attracts me?
Whatever it is, it's the most thrilling thing that has ever happened to
me, and I don't want it to ever end.

Yes, Lord. I know You have a plan for me, much better than anything
I could work out by myself. Maybe he is part of Your plan. Or maybe this
love I feel now is only for today.

Whatever happens in the future, I feel great today. The happy feeling inside me right now has to be a gift from You—thank You! Thank You, Lord Jesus, for caring about my todays and about my future. Because I am important to You, I can enjoy today and still learn and plan and think and grow. Help me to live my life for You. Work in my life to make me into the faithful wife and good mother You desire for me to become someday. I know I can leave my future in Your loving hands.

Decisions

We live by faith, not by sight (2 Corinthians 5:7).

Ever since I can remember, I have longed to be grown up. But how do I know I won't become trapped by my mistakes? Sometimes I think being alone is the only way to keep from being hurt. I see steady couples torn by jealousy and hurt feelings, marriages ripped apart, families who do nothing but yell at each other. Is love really worth the risk?

You think so, don't You, Jesus? You allowed Yourself to be tortured, deserted by friends, misunderstood—for love's sake. You were willing to suffer anything to make the Church—all of us—your Bride. I know I can always count on Your love for me, on Your unchanging presence in my life. Troubles may come, but I cling to the belief that You will show me how to love and be loved.

Although I have made many mistakes, You have forgiven and restored me. You have taught me how to choose friends and how to be a friend. Guide me now as I learn how to be a loving person. Help me to overcome temptation and to avoid the entrapment that can happen by listening to the lies about sexuality that abound in our culture. Make me into the godly woman You would have me be.

Not Far Enough?

For this reason He had to be made like His brothers in every way. . . . Because He Himself suffered when He was tempted, He is able to help those who are being tempted (Hebrews 2:17–18).

Does everyone else really do it? Is it as great as they claim? Am I missing something wonderful by waiting? Lord, when they joke about the boys they've been with, I don't know what to say. Usually I pretend not to understand their questions—or I kid around with them, say something they can take any way they like. Either way, I feel like a fool.

I like boys, Lord. I'm pretty sure that my sex drive is as strong as anybody's. And sometimes I feel very unwilling to wait any longer. I want it *now.*

What kinds of feelings did You experience, Jesus, as You were growing up? I have trouble picturing You struggling with problems like mine. Yet I know You are human like us, along with being true God. How did You deal with temptations?

Help me, Lord, to remember You understand how I feel, so I can talk and question and confess freely to You—and get Your power to act in Your way. Guide and strengthen me, Jesus, for You are my hope, my Lord and Savior. Amen.

Glossary

Abortion (a-BOR-shun) The premature termination of a pregnancy, in which the fetus is killed.

Abstinence (AB-stin-ens) Voluntarily avoiding something. In sexual connotation, refraining from sexual activity.

Adolescence (ad-uh-LES-sens) The period of life between puberty and adulthood.

Adultery (a-DULL-ter-ee) Sexual intercourse with a person who is legally married to someone else. The term is often used to describe any sexual intercourse outside of marriage.

AIDS (Acquired Immune Deficiency Syndrome) A life-threatening viral disease most commonly transmitted through blood or semen or both either by sexual contact or by use of dirty needles in "shooting" drugs.

Amnion (AM-nee-on) The thin membrane that forms the sac of water surrounding the fetus within the uterus. Contains amniotic fluid in which the fetus is immersed for protection against shocks and jolts.

Androgen (AN-dro-jen) A hormone that influences growth and the sex drive in the male. Produces masculine secondary sex characteristics (voice changes, hair growth, etc.).

Anus (AY-nuss) The opening at the base of the buttocks through which solid waste is eliminated from the intestines.

Artificial Insemination The medical procedure of injecting semen into the vagina close to the cervix by artificial means; can enable pregnancy in spite of fertility problems.

AZT A drug that, for some people, slows the development of AIDS.

Birth Control See *Contraception*.

Bisexual (by-SECKS-shoo-al) A person who has a sexual interest in both sexes.

Bladder (BLAD-er) A sac in the pelvic region where urine is stored until elimination.

Breech Birth The birth position when the baby's feet or buttocks instead of his or her head appear first in the birth canal.

Caesarean Section (si-SAIR-ee-an) (Caesarean Birth; "C" Section) Delivery of a baby by surgical incision through the abdomen into the uterus.

Castration (kas-TRAY-shun) Removal of the sex glands—the testicles in men, the ovaries in women.

Cervix (SER-viks) The narrow, lower part of the uterus, which opens into the deep portion of the vagina.

Chancre (SHANG-ker) A small sore or ulcerated area, usually on the genitals, which can be an early symptom of syphilis.

Chastity (CHAS-ti-tee) Cultivating a life of purity whether single or married.

Chlamydia (kla-MID-ee-ah) See *Sexually Transmitted Disease*.

Chromosome (KRO-mo-soam) One of the more or less rodlike bodies found in the nucleus of all cells, containing the heredity factors or genes. Twenty-two pairs of chromosomes account for a person's hereditary characteristics. The twenty-third pair determines sex. See *X Chromosome* and *Y Chromosome*.

Cilia (SIL-ee-uh) (plural of cilium) Tiny hairlike process often forming part of a fringe, especially on a cell, capable of lashing movement—tiny eyelash-like hairs moving something forward.

Circumcision (ser-kum-SIZH-un) Surgical removal of the foreskin or prepuce of the penis. Originally a Jewish rite performed as a sign of reception into their faith; now generally performed for purposes of cleanliness.

Climax See *Orgasm*.

Clitoris (KLIT-or-is) A small, highly sensitive female organ located just above the urethra.

Coitus (KO-i-tus) (Copulation) Sexual intercourse between male and female, in which the penis is inserted into the vagina.

Conception (kon-SEP-shun) (Impregnation) Penetration of the ovum (female egg cell) by a sperm, resulting in development of an embryo—new life.

Condom See *Contraception*.

Congenital (kon-JEN-i-tal) A condition existing from birth. May or may not be inherited.

Contraception (kon-trah-SEP-shun) (Birth control) The prevention of conception by use of devices, drugs, or other means in sexual intercourse.

Cowper's glands Small glands lying alongside the male urethra that secrete part of the seminal fluid.

Cunnilingus (kun-i-LING-us) The act of applying the mouth or tongue to the vulva to stimulate the female.

Delivery The process of giving birth.

Douching (dooshing) The cleansing of the vagina with a stream of liquid solution or water.

Ejaculation (ee-jack-yoo-LAY-shun) The discharge of semen from the penis.

Embryo (EM-bree-oh) The unborn in its earliest stages of development. In humans, the fertilized ovum during the first eight weeks of its growth.

Endometrium (en-doh-MEE-tree-um) The lining of the uterus, which thickens and fills with blood in preparation for a fertilized ovum.

Epididymis (ep-ah-DID-i-miss) The mass of tiny coils connecting the testicles with the sperm duct.

Erection (ee-RECK-shun) The enlargement and hardening of the penis or clitoris as tissues fill with blood, usually during sexual excitement.

Erogenous Zone (i-RAH-jen-us) Any area of the body that is sexually sensitive or stimulating such as mouth, lips, breasts, nipples, and genitals.

Erotic (ee-RAH-tik) Sexually stimulating.

Estrogen (ESS-tro-jen) A hormone that affects functioning of the menstrual cycle and produces female secondary sex characteristics (breast development, widened hips, etc.).

Exhibitionist (ex-i-BISH-un-ist) A person who compulsively exposes his or her sex organs in public.

Extramarital (ex-tra-MARE-i-tal) "Outside of marriage"; often used to refer to illicit sexual intercourse, i.e., "extramarital affair."

Fallopian Tube (fa-LOW-pee-an) The tube through which the egg passes from the ovary to the uterus.

Fellatio (fel-LAY-show) The act of applying the mouth or tongue to the penis to stimulate the male.

Fertility The ability to reproduce.

Fertilization Penetration of the female ovum by a single sperm, resulting in conception.

Fetus (FEE-tuss) The unborn child from the third month after conception until birth.

Follicle (FALL-ick-l) A vesicle in the ovary that contains a developing egg surrounded by a covering of cells. A mature follicle ruptures during ovulation to release an egg.

Foreplay The beginning stage of sexual intercourse, during which partners may kiss, caress, and touch each other in order to achieve full sexual arousal.

Foreskin The loose skin covering the tip of the penis, removed during circumcision. Also called the prepuce (PREE-pus).

Fornication (for-ni-KAY-shun) Sexual intercourse between unmarried men and women.

Genes (jeans) The carriers for hereditary traits in chromosomes.

Genital Herpes See *Sexually Transmitted Disease.*

Genitalia (jen-i-TAIL-ya) (Genitals; Genital Organs) Visible reproductive or sex organs. Usually denotes vagina, vulva, and clitoris in females and the penis and testicles in males.

Gestation (jes-TAY-shun) The period from conception to birth, approximately nine months for humans.

Glans (glanz) The head of the penis exposed when the foreskin is pushed back or after circumcision.

Gonorrhea (gon-er-EE-uh) See *Sexually Transmitted Disease.*

Gynecologist (guy-na-KOLL-o-jist) A physician who specializes in the treatment of female sexual and reproductive organs.

Heredity (her-ED-it-ee) Traits, characteristics, or diseases transmitted from parents to children.

Heterosexual (het-er-o-SECK-shoo-al) One who is sexually attracted to or sexually active with persons of the other sex.

HIV (Human Immunodeficiency Virus) The virus that causes AIDS.

Homosexual (ho-mo-SECK-shoo-al) One who is sexually attracted to or sexually active with persons of one's own sex.

Hormone (HOR-moan) A chemical substance, produced by an endocrine gland, that has a particular effect on the function of other organs in the body.

Human Papilloma Virus (HPV) (pap-il-LO-ma) See *Sexually Transmitted Disease.*

Hymen (HIGH-men) A thin membrane that partially closes the entrance to the vagina.

Hysterectomy (hiss-ter-ECK-toh-mee) Surgical removal of the uterus. May include removal of one or both ovaries (oophorectomy).

Impotent (IM-po-tent) Unable to achieve or maintain erection of the penis during sexual intercourse. Impotence is a type of male sexual dysfunction that has many causes.

Incest (IN-sest) Sexual intercourse between close relatives such as father and daughter, mother and son, or brother and sister.

Intercourse, Sexual See *Coitus*.

Jock Itch A fungus infection causing skin irritation in the genital area.

Labor The birth stage in which the cervix gradually dilates, allowing strong contractions of the uterine muscles to push the baby through the vagina and out of the mother's body.

Lesbian (LEZ-be-an) A female homosexual.

Libido (li-BEE-doe) See *Sex Drive*.

Masochism (MASS-o-kizm) Cruelty to self; receiving sexual pleasure from having pain inflicted or by being harshly dominated.

Masturbation (mass-ter-BAY-shun) Self-stimulation of one's sex organs, often to the point of orgasm.

Menarche (MEN-arc-ee) The onset of the menstrual cycle in a girl.

Menopause (MEN-o-pawz) (Change of Life; Climacteric) The end of menstruation in women, usually between the ages of 45 and 55.

Menstruation (men-stroo-AY-shun) The discharge through the vagina of blood and endometrium from the uterus. This menstrual "period" usually occurs every 28–30 days in females, between puberty and menopause.

Miscarriage The natural expulsion of the fetus from the uterus before it is mature enough to survive, usually due to some abnormal development.

Nocturnal Emission (nok-TER-nal ee-MISH-un) (Wet Dream) Involuntary male erection and ejaculation during sleep.

Obstetrician (ob-ste-TRISH-un) A physician who specializes in the care of women during pregnancy and childbirth, and immediately thereafter.

Oral Sex See *Cunnilingus; Fellatio.*

Orgasm (OR-gazm) (Climax) The peak of excitement in sexual activity.

Ovaries (OH-va-rees) The two female sex glands found on either side of the uterus, in which the ova (egg cells) are formed. They also produce hormones that influence female body characteristics.

Ovulation (ah-vyoo-LAY-shun) Release of the mature (ripe) ovum from the ovary to the fallopian tube.

Ovum (OH-vum) (Plural: ova) Female reproductive cell (egg) found in the ovary. After fertilization by a male sperm, the human egg develops into an embryo and then a fetus.

Penis (PEE-nis) Male sex organ through which semen is discharged and urine is passed.

Pituitary (pih-TOO-it-air-ee) A gland at the base of the brain that controls functions of all the other ductless glands, especially sex glands, adrenals, and thyroid.

Placenta (pluh-SEN-ta) The sponge-like organ that connects the fetus to the lining of the uterus by means of the umbilical cord. It serves to feed the fetus and to dispose of waste. Expelled from the uterus after the birth of a child (afterbirth).

Pornography (por-NOG-raf-ee) Literature, motion pictures, art, or other means of expression that, without any concern for personal or moral values, intend simply to be sexually arousing.

Pregnancy (PREG-nan-see) Period from conception to birth; the condition of having a developing embryo or fetus within the female body.

Prenatal (pree-NAY-tal) Before birth.

Progesterone (pro-JES-te-roan) (Progestin) The female "pregnancy hormone" that prepares the uterus to receive the fertilized ovum.

Promiscuous (pro-MISS-kyoo-us) Engaging in sexual intercourse with many persons; engaging in casual sexual relationships.

Prostate (PRAH-state) Male gland that surrounds the urethra and neck of the bladder and secretes part of the seminal fluid.

Prostitute (PRAH-sti-toot) An individual who engages in sexual activity for money.

Puberty (PYOO-ber-tee) The period of rapid development that marks the end of childhood; sex organs mature and produce either eggs or sperm; the girl becomes a young woman and the boy a young man.

Pubic (PYOO-bik) Regarding the lower part of the abdominal area, where hair grows in a triangular patch.

Rape (rayp) Forcible sexual intercourse with a person who does not consent.

Rectum (RECK-tum) The lower end of the large intestine, ending at the anus.

Rhythm Method See *Contraception*.

Sadism (SADE-izm) Cruelty; receiving sexual pleasure by inflicting pain on the sexual partner.

Safe Period The interval in the menstrual cycle when the female is presumably not ovulating and therefore unable to become pregnant.

Safe Sex The claim that using a condom will prevent STDs. Much medical research disproves the claim. The only truly safe sex is to remain a virgin until married and then have intercourse only with an uninfected spouse.

Scrotum (SKRO-tum) The sac of skin suspended between the male's legs that contains the testicles.

Semen (SEE-men) (Seminal Fluid; Seminal Emission) The fluid made up of sperm, secretions from the seminal vesicles, prostate and Cowper's glands, and the epididymis. Ejaculated through the penis when the male reaches orgasm.

Seminal Vesicles (SEM-i-nal VESS-i-cals) Two storage pouches for sperm (which is produced in the testicles). Located on either side of the prostate, they are attached to and open into the sperm ducts.

Sex Drive (Libido) The desire for sexual activity.

Sex, Oral See *Cunnilingus; Fellatio.*

Sex Organs Commonly refers to the male penis and female vagina.

Sexual Dysfunction Term used to describe problems in sexual performance, which could be physical or emotional in nature.

Sexual Intercourse See *Coitus.*

Sexually Transmitted Disease (STD) Any of a variety of contagious diseases contracted almost entirely by sexual intercourse. Some of the most common are AIDS, chlamydia, genital herpes, gonorrhea, human papilloma virus (HPV), trichomoniasis, and syphilis.

Sperm The male reproductive cell(s), produced in the testicles, having the capacity to fertilize the female ova, resulting in pregnancy.

Spermatic Duct (sper-MAT-ik dukt) (Vas Deferens) The tube in the male through which sperm passes from the epididymis to the seminal vesicles and urethra.

Spermatic Cord The tube in the male by which the testicle is suspended; contains the sperm ducts, veins, and nerves.

Spermicide See *Contraception.*

Sterility (ster-ILL-it-ee) The inability to reproduce.

Sterilization (ster-ill-ih-ZAY-shun) A procedure by which a male or female is rendered unable to produce children but can still engage in sexual intercourse. Some of the most common surgical methods include:

Laparoscopic Sterilization (la-pa-RO-sko-pic) Tiny incisions in the abdomen, through which the fallopian tubes are cut or cauterized. Also called "Band-Aid Sterilization."

Tubal Ligation (TOO-bul lie-GAY-shun) The surgeon cuts and ties the ends of both fallopian tubes after making a larger incision in the abdomen or by going through the vagina.

Vasectomy (vas-ECK-toe-mee) The male sperm-carrying duct is cut, part is removed, and the ends tied.

Syphilis (SIF-i-lis) See *Sexually Transmitted Disease*.

Testicles (TESS-ti-klz) (Testes) The two male sex glands that produce sperm. They are suspended within a sac of skin between the legs, behind the penis.

Testosterone (tes-TOSS-ter-own) Male sex hormone produced by the testes; causes and maintains male secondary sex characteristics (voice change, hair growth, etc.).

Transsexual (trans-SECK-shoo-al) One who feels psychologically like a member of the other sex and may seek "sex change" surgery to achieve the outward appearance of the other sex.

Transvestite One who has a compulsion to dress in the clothing of the other sex.

Trichomoniasis (trick-uh-muh-NY-uh-sis) See *Sexually Transmitted Disease*.

Umbilical Cord (um-BILL-i-kal) The cord connecting the fetus to the placenta, through which the fetus receives nourishment.

Urethra (yoo-REE-thra) The duct through which urine passes from the bladder and is eliminated from the body.

Urologist (yoo-RAHL-i-jist) A physician who specializes in treating urinary tract problems of both sexes, as well as the genital tract of males.

Uterus (YOO-ter-us) The small, muscular, pear-shaped female organ in which the fetus develops; has the ability to expand to accommodate the growing child (children).

Vagina (vuh-JY-na) (Birth Canal) The canal in the female body between the uterus and the vulva that receives the penis during intercourse; the canal through which an infant passes at birth.

Vas Deferens (VAS DEF-er-enz) See *Spermatic Duct.*

Vasectomy See *Sterilization.*

Virgin (VER-jin) A person who has never had sexual intercourse.

Vulva (VUL-va) The female's external sex organs, including the labia majora and labia minora, the outer and inner folds of skin (lips) surrounding the vagina, and the clitoris.

Wet Dream See *Nocturnal Emission.*

Womb (WOOM) See *Uterus.*

X Chromosome A chromosome that determines sex, present in all female ova and in one-half of a male's sperm. If the egg is fertilized by a sperm having an X chromosome, a female will be conceived (XX).

Y Chromosome A sex-determining chromosome present in one-half of a male's sperm. If an ovum is fertilized by a sperm with a Y chromosome, a male will be conceived (XY).